# Skills
# for
# Effective
# Writing
# 4

CAMBRIDGE
UNIVERSITY PRESS

# CAMBRIDGE
## UNIVERSITY PRESS

Cambridge University Press
32 Avenue of the Americas, New York, NY 10013-2473, USA

www.cambridge.org
Information on this title: www.cambridge.org/9781107613577

First published 2013
5th printing 2014

Printed in Hong Kong, China, by Golden Cup Printing Company Limited

*A catalog record for this publication is available from the British Library.*

ISBN 978-1-107-61357-7 Student's Book

The publisher wishes to acknowledge the contributions of the following writers:
Laurie Blass, Susan Hills, Hilary Hodge, Kathryn O'Dell, and Mari Vargo.

Art direction, book design, cover design, editorial management, layout services,
and photo research: Hyphen S.A.

Cover image: ©Ingmar Bjork/Shutterstock.com

Photography: 2 ©Todd Klassy/Shutterstock.com; 6 ©Andresr/Shutterstock.com;
10 ©wong yu liang/ Shutterstock.com; 14 ©oorka/Shutterstock.com; 18 ©Blend
Images/Shutterstock.com; 22 ©Andresr/Shutterstock.com; 26 ©Rob Marmion/
Shutterstock.com; 30 ©iStockphoto.com/track5; 34 ©Andy Dean Photography/
Shutterstock.com; 38 ©iStockphoto/Thinkstock.com; 42 ©Stephen Coburn/
Shutterstock.com; 46 ©alvarez/Shutterstock.com; 50 ©Bogdan Wankowicz/
Shutterstock.com; 54 ©Catalin Petolea/Shutterstock.com; 58 ©lenetstan/
Shutterstock.com; 62 ©Kochneva Tetyana/Shutterstock.com; 66 ©Tatiana
Popover/Shutterstock.com; 70 ©iStockphoto.com/Kuzma; 74 ©iStockphoto.com/
apomares; 78 ©iStockphoto.com/xavierarnau

# Skills for Effective Writing 4

CAMBRIDGE
UNIVERSITY PRESS

# Contents

Discrete writing skills, such as creating topic sentences and recognizing irrelevant information, are critical for good writers. This 4-level series teaches these skills and offers extensive practice opportunities.

## SKILL PRESENTATION

Each unit teaches a single discrete writing skill, helping students focus their attention on developing the skill fully.

## OVER TO YOU

Following instruction, students are eased into the skill's application, facilitating their understanding of exactly how each skill works.

When students master these skills, all of their writing improves. This allows teachers to focus their time and feedback on the content of student work.

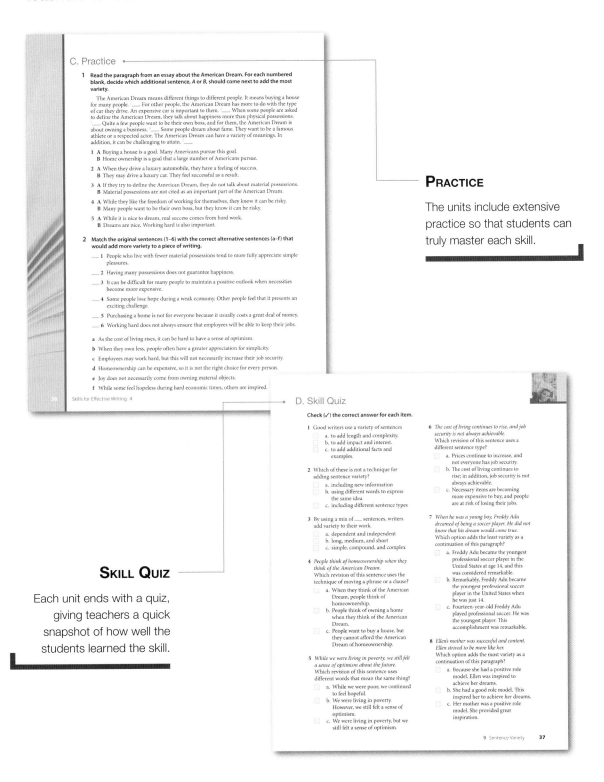

**C. Practice**

1 Read the paragraph from an essay about the American Dream. For each numbered blank, decide which additional sentence, A or B, should come next to add the most variety.

The American Dream means different things to different people. It means buying a house for many people. ___. For other people, the American Dream has more to do with the type of car they drive. An expensive car is important to them. ___. When some people are asked to define the American Dream, they talk about happiness more than physical possessions. ___. Quite a few people want to be their own boss, and for them, the American Dream is about owning a business. ___. Some people dream about fame. They want to be a famous athlete or a respected actor. The American Dream can have a variety of meanings. In addition, it can be challenging to attain. ___.

1 A Buying a house is a goal. Many Americans pursue this goal.
  B Home ownership is a goal that a large number of Americans pursue.

2 A When they drive a luxury automobile, they have a feeling of success.
  B They may drive a luxury car. They feel successful as a result.

3 A If they try to define the American Dream, they do not talk about material possessions.
  B Material possessions are not cited as an important part of the American Dream.

4 A While they like the freedom of working for themselves, they know it can be risky.
  B Many people want to be their own boss, but they know it can be risky.

5 A While it is nice to dream, real success comes from hard work.
  B Dreams are nice. Working hard is also important.

2 Match the original sentences (1–6) with the correct alternative sentences (a–f) that would add more variety to a piece of writing.

___ 1 People who live with fewer material possessions tend to more fully appreciate simple pleasures.

___ 2 Having many possessions does not guarantee happiness.

___ 3 It can be difficult for many people to maintain a positive outlook when necessities become more expensive.

___ 4 Some people lose hope during a weak economy. Other people feel that it presents an exciting challenge.

___ 5 Purchasing a home is not for everyone because it usually costs a great deal of money.

___ 6 Working hard does not always ensure that employees will be able to keep their jobs.

a As the cost of living rises, it can be hard to have a sense of optimism.

b When they own less, people often have a greater appreciation for simplicity.

c Employees may work hard, but this will not necessarily increase their job security.

d Homeownership can be expensive, so it is not the right choice for every person.

e Joy does not necessarily come from owning material objects.

f While some feel hopeless during hard economic times, others are inspired.

Skills for Effective Writing 4 — 36

**PRACTICE**

The units include extensive practice so that students can truly master each skill.

**D. Skill Quiz**

Check (✓) the correct answer for each item.

1 Good writers use a variety of sentences
  ☐ a. to add length and complexity.
  ☐ b. to add impact and interest.
  ☐ c. to add additional facts and examples.

2 Which of these is not a technique for adding sentence variety?
  ☐ a. including new information
  ☐ b. using different words to express the same idea
  ☐ c. including different sentence types

3 By using a mix of ___ sentences, writers add variety to their work.
  ☐ a. dependent and independent
  ☐ b. long, medium, and short
  ☐ c. simple, compound, and complex

4 People think of homeownership when they think of the American Dream.
  Which revision of this sentence uses the technique of moving a phrase or a clause?
  ☐ a. When they think of the American Dream, people think of homeownership.
  ☐ b. People think of owning a home when they think of the American Dream.
  ☐ c. People want to buy a house, but they cannot afford the American Dream of homeownership.

5 While we were living in poverty, we still felt a sense of optimism about the future.
  Which revision of this sentence uses different words that mean the same thing?
  ☐ a. While we were poor, we continued to feel hopeful.
  ☐ b. We were living in poverty. However, we still felt a sense of optimism.
  ☐ c. We were living in poverty, but we still felt a sense of optimism.

6 The cost of living continues to rise, and job security is not always achievable.
  Which revision of this sentence uses a different sentence type?
  ☐ a. Prices continue to increase, and not everyone has job security.
  ☐ b. The cost of living continues to rise; in addition, job security is not always achievable.
  ☐ c. Necessary items are becoming more expensive to buy, and people are at risk of losing their jobs.

7 When he was a young boy, Freddy Adu dreamed of being a soccer player. He did not know that his dream would come true.
  Which option adds the least variety as a continuation of this paragraph?
  ☐ a. Freddy Adu became the youngest professional soccer player in the United States at age 14, and this was considered remarkable.
  ☐ b. Remarkably, Freddy Adu became the youngest professional soccer player in the United States when he was just 14.
  ☐ c. Fourteen-year-old Freddy Adu played professional soccer. He was the youngest player. This accomplishment was remarkable.

8 Ellen's mother was successful and content. Ellen strived to be more like her.
  Which option adds the most variety as a continuation of this paragraph?
  ☐ a. Because she had a positive role model, Ellen was inspired to achieve her dreams.
  ☐ b. She had a good role model. This inspired her to achieve her dreams.
  ☐ c. Her mother was a positive role model. She provided great inspiration.

9 Sentence Variety  37

**SKILL QUIZ**

Each unit ends with a quiz, giving teachers a quick snapshot of how well the students learned the skill.

## THE ENVIRONMENT AND YOU

### CONNECTING TO THE THEME

**How "environmentally friendly" are you?**

How do you get to school or work each day?
  **A** I take the subway.   **B** I always drive.   **C** I ride my bike.

What do you use to take notes on in class?
  **A** I use a notebook made from 100 percent recycled paper.   **B** I use expensive, white, lined paper.
  **C** I use my laptop.

What kinds of bags do you use at the grocery store?
  **A** I use paper bags that I recycle.   **B** I use plastic bags that I throw away.
  **C** I use a canvas bag that I re-use each day.

*Mostly As: there's room for improvement! Mostly Bs: you're not environmentally friendly at all. Mostly Cs: you're very environmentally friendly.*

## A. Skill Presentation

Some of the most common mistakes in writing are using sentence fragments, run-on sentences, and comma splices.

A **sentence fragment** is the result of
- a sentence missing either a subject or a verb.
- a sentence not expressing a complete idea.
- a dependent clause being used on its own without an independent clause.

Look at these sentence fragments and how they can be corrected.

Is a major problem. ✗ (missing a subject)
**Water pollution** is a major problem. ✓

Environmentalists work the effects of pollution. ✗ (doesn't express a complete idea)
Environmentalists work **to decrease** the effects of pollution. ✓

Because it affects the whole world. ✗ (missing an independent clause)
**Pollution is a global problem** because it affects the whole world. ✓

A **run-on sentence** has two or more independent clauses that are connected without a comma or a conjunction. Look at this sentence and how it can be corrected.

Air pollution can cause health problems it can make existing problems worse. ✗
Air pollution can cause health problems**.** It can make existing problems worse. ✓
Air pollution can cause health problems**, and** it can make existing problems worse. ✓

A **comma splice** has two or more independent clauses that are connected with a comma, but without a conjunction. Look at this sentence and how it can be corrected.

People may have access to water, this water may not be clean. ✗
People may have access to water, **but** this water may not be clean. ✓

# B. Over to You

**1** Read the sentences and decide why they are incorrect. Write *SF* for Sentence Fragment, *RO* for Run-On Sentence, or *CS* for Comma Splice.

___ **1** Polluted air can cause health problems it can shorten lives.

___ **2** Polluted water may be unsafe, experts advise against drinking it.

___ **3** Pollution becoming a crisis in a large number of regions throughout the world.

**2** Read each item in the chart, and decide if it is a correct sentence, a sentence fragment, a run-on sentence, or a comma splice. Check (✓) the box in the correct column.

| | CORRECT SENTENCE | SENTENCE FRAGMENT | RUN-ON SENTENCE | COMMA SPLICE |
|---|---|---|---|---|
| 1. Water pollution is a problem people using too much water is also a problem. | | | | |
| 2. People should take steps to conserve water. | | | | |
| 3. Should follow these guidelines to conserve water. | | | | |
| 4. When people brush their teeth. | | | | |
| 5. People should check for leaks, they should have them fixed. | | | | |
| 6. Some people encourage others to use. | | | | |
| 7. People can also help keep water clean. | | | | |
| 8. They can chemicals to a collection site. | | | | |
| 9. Collection sites safely get rid of chemicals this helps keep water clean. | | | | |
| 10. Some chemicals may pollute drinking water if they are not thrown away properly. | | | | |

## CHECK!

**1** A _____ _____ does not express a complete idea. It may be missing a subject or a _____, or it may be a dependent clause missing an _____ clause.

**2** Two or more _____ clauses joined together without a comma or a conjunction results in a _____ _____.

**3** Two or more independent clauses connected with a comma but without a conjunction is a _____ _____.

# C. Practice

**1  Read each pair of sentences. Check (✓) the correct sentence.**

**1** ☐ a. Noise pollution does not harm animals it can cause them to leave their homes.
☐ b. Noise pollution does not harm animals, but it can cause them to leave their homes.

**2** ☐ a. Light pollution does not harm people in immediately obvious ways, but it can be very irritating.
☐ b. Light pollution does not harm people in immediately obvious ways, it can be very irritating.

**3** ☐ a. Smog used to mean the combination of smoke and fog, today it refers to polluted air.
☐ b. Smog used to mean the combination of smoke and fog, but today it refers to polluted air.

**4** ☐ a. The word smog was first used in the 1900s, but it had a different meaning then.
☐ b. The word smog was first used in the 1900s it had a different meaning then.

**5** ☐ a. Soil pollution contaminates the ground, and it may prevent plants from growing.
☐ b. Soil pollution contaminates the ground it may prevent plants from growing.

**6** ☐ a. Smog causes many health problems the impact is often immediate.
☐ b. Smog causes many health problems, and the impact is often immediate.

**2  Read the sentence fragments and a student's explanations of what is wrong. Write C if the student's explanation is correct or I if it is incorrect.**

**1** Carbon dioxide a gas produced by the body.
___ "This sentence fragment is missing a verb."

**2** When it comes from other sources.
___ "This sentence fragment is a dependent clause not connected to an independent clause."

**3** Many industries require.
___ "This sentence fragment does not express a complete idea because it is missing an object."

**4** Contains significant amounts of carbon dioxide.
___ "This sentence fragment is a dependent clause not connected to an independent clause."

**5** Causes both short-term and long-term damage.
___ "This sentence fragment is missing a subject."

**6** Air pollution irritating to the eyes, nose, and throat.
___ "This sentence fragment is missing a verb."

**7** Other short-term problems include.
___ "This sentence fragment is missing a subject."

# D. Skill Quiz

**Check (✓) the correct answer for each item.**

**1** One type of a sentence fragment is
- [ ] a. two independent clauses connected without a comma.
- [ ] b. an independent clause with a subject and a complete verb.
- [ ] c. a dependent clause not connected to an independent clause.

**2** A run-on sentence is
- [ ] a. two independent clauses connected without a comma.
- [ ] b. two independent clauses connected only with a comma.
- [ ] c. a dependent clause not connected to an independent clause.

**3** A comma splice is
- [ ] a. two independent clauses connected only by a comma.
- [ ] b. a dependent clause not connected to an independent clause.
- [ ] c. a sentence without a verb.

**4** Choose the sentence fragment.
- [ ] a. Some experts say too many trees are cut down every year.
- [ ] b. Because the new trees do not grow quickly enough to replace those that have been cut down.
- [ ] c. Environmentalists argue that people use too much paper, it damages forests.

**5** Choose the run-on sentence.
- [ ] a. Homes are larger than in the past, and we are using more trees to build them.
- [ ] b. Homes are larger than in the past, we are using more trees to build them.
- [ ] c. Homes are larger than in the past we are using more trees to build them.

**6** Choose the comma splice.
- [ ] a. Noise pollution draws less attention because it doesn't harm the environment in immediately obvious ways.
- [ ] b. Noise levels are increasing in large cities, this causes birds to leave.
- [ ] c. The noise from machines used to chop down trees is driving many animals from the forest.

**7** *Environmentalists and other concerned citizens investigate.*
This sentence fragment is missing
- [ ] a. a subject.
- [ ] b. a verb.
- [ ] c. an object.

**8** *Pollution causing a variety of problems throughout the planet.*
This sentence fragment is missing
- [ ] a. a subject.
- [ ] b. a verb.
- [ ] c. a dependent clause.

**9** *Is possible to reduce pollution with the cooperation of governments and private industry.*
This sentence fragment is missing
- [ ] a. a subject.
- [ ] b. a verb.
- [ ] c. an object.

**10** *If we do not do something soon.*
This sentence fragment is missing
- [ ] a. a subject.
- [ ] b. a verb.
- [ ] c. an independent clause.

## Connectors 1: Connectors for Cause and Effect Writing

### CONNECTING TO THE THEME

One reason advertisements are so effective is that they contain slogans – catchy words and phrases that make you remember a company's product. How many of these slogans do you recognize?

[1]"Just do it!"   [2]"Don't leave home without it."   [3]"Betcha can't eat just one."   [4]"Think different."
[5]"It keeps going, and going, and going, and going."   [6]"Reach out and touch someone."

*1 Nike, 2 American Express, 3 Lays potato chips, 4 Apple, 5 Energizer batteries, 6 AT&T*

## A. Skill Presentation

A cause–effect essay explains the reasons why an event or situation happens (cause), or it gives the results of an event or situation (effect). There are certain connectors you can use to link your ideas in a cause–effect essay and make your writing coherent, or clear and smooth.

Some connectors that help show reasons or causes are *one reason is*, *another reason is*, *one cause is*, and *the most important cause is*. These words and phrases show connections between ideas in different sentences. Other connectors that show reasons are *because*, *because of*, *since*, and *due to*. These words can help link ideas within a sentence.

Read this paragraph from a cause–effect essay that gives reasons why people enjoy bargaining. Look at the **connectors** the writer has used to show cause.

> Throughout the world, many people enjoy bargaining. **One reason is** that people feel successful when they pay a lower price. They feel a sense of accomplishment **since** they are able to achieve the goal of paying less than the ticketed price. **Another reason** many people enjoy bargaining is **because** they feel that they are saving money.

Connectors that help show results or effects in a cause–effect essay include *as a result, for this reason, consequently,* and *therefore*. Other connectors that show results include: *so* and *so that*.

# B. Over to You

**1** **Read the paragraph and underline the three connectors the writer has used to show effect.**

Some people make purchases for emotional reasons, and this can have negative effects. For instance, people may buy products so that they feel better when they are sad. As a result, they may feel better, but the improvement in mood is likely to last for only a short period of time. Sometimes people buy products to feel important. Consequently, they may spend more money than they have.

**2** **Read each sentence in the chart, and decide if the words in bold show a reason or a result. Check (✓) the box in the correct column.**

| | SHOW A REASON | SHOW A RESULT |
|---|---|---|
| 1. Bargaining is acceptable in India. **Therefore, store owners often raise their prices.** | | |
| 2. Many teenagers use the Internet frequently. **For this reason, they constantly see advertisements.** | | |
| 3. Companies have sales **because many consumers do not like to buy full-priced items.** | | |
| 4. Stores have sales to make more money. Products are cheaper, **so people often buy more items.** | | |
| 5. A company must understand the product's target market **since developing successful products is challenging.** | | |
| 6. Targeting a specific market is important. **One reason is that it keeps advertising costs low.** | | |
| 7. When people are bargaining, they often walk away from the seller. **Consequently, the seller thinks he may lose the customer, and he will lower the price.** | | |
| 8. Internet advertisements are often effective **due to the fact that many people have access to computers.** | | |

## CHECK!

Use connectors when you write to link ideas and add coherence to your writing. Here are some useful connectors for cause–effect essays.

**1** To show _____:
*One reason / cause*
*Another reason / cause*
*The most important cause*
*because (of)*
*since*
*due to*

**2** To show _____:
*As a result,*
*For this reason,*
*Consequently,*
*Therefore,*
*so*
*so (that)*

# C. Practice

**1   Circle the correct answer for each item.**

1   Companies often study consumer behavior before they create advertisements. They develop ads that appeal to their target market's interests *because of* | *so* their effective research.

2   People liked the shoe company's slogan "Own Your Power." They bought the shoes *due to* | *because* they could feel powerful.

3   Companies know that people are more interested in food when they are hungry. *Another reason is* | *For this reason*, food companies often advertise snacks on TV late in the afternoon.

4   Consumers are more likely to purchase products that celebrities promote. *One reason for this* | *One result* is that they feel a sense of connection to that person if they own the same product.

5   Companies collect data about the effectiveness of an advertisement *consequently* | *due to the fact* that they want to know how well their advertisements work.

6   If a famous athlete wears a certain type of shoe, some people think this shoe will make them better at sports. *Therefore,* | *Due to* athletes can help a company increase its sales.

7   Some people buy items that they don't need *because* | *due to* they have been influenced by successful advertising.

8   Some products are advertised in movies. This is called "product placement." It can be a successful strategy *since* | *therefore* consumers connect the product with the movie star.

**2   Read the beginning of the paragraph, and number the sentences in the correct order to complete the paragraph.**

Advertisements directed at young children are often very effective, but their effects are not always positive. For instance, children want to have products they see even if they do not need them.

____ As a result, they may develop an addiction to unhealthy foods.

____ Consequently, they often bother their parents until their parents buy the products.

____ Therefore, parents and children should discuss the advertisements they see on television.

____ Another reason these advertisements may be harmful is that children want the unhealthy foods they see on TV.

# D. Skill Quiz

**Check (✓) the correct answer for each item.**

1  What do connectors do in an essay?
- [ ] a. state the topic
- [ ] b. link ideas
- [ ] c. make sentences parallel

2  What is the purpose of a cause–effect essay?
- [ ] a. to show results or effects
- [ ] b. to give readers opinions about two topics
- [ ] c. to show the order of importance of points

3  Which connectors show causes?
- [ ] a. first, second
- [ ] b. another reason is, so that
- [ ] c. for example, for instance

4  Which connectors show effects?
- [ ] a. one reason is, because of
- [ ] b. next, finally
- [ ] c. therefore, consequently

5  Which sentence shows a cause?
- [ ] a. People should not bargain in American restaurants because it is not culturally acceptable.
- [ ] b. Consequently, no one bargains in restaurants.
- [ ] c. Therefore, pay the bill without trying to bargain.

6  Which sentence shows a result?
- [ ] a. First, a company should consider what affects people's decisions to buy products.
- [ ] b. The first reason is that people buy creams to improve their skin.
- [ ] c. Therefore, the sales of beauty products increased.

7  Choose the sentence which most likely follows this one: *The company advertised their product more successfully.*
- [ ] a. One reason was to decrease the cost of advertising.
- [ ] b. As a result, their sales figures increased.
- [ ] c. For this reason, they also advertised on the television.

8  Choose the sentence which most likely follows this one: *Bargaining is common in Cairo.*
- [ ] a. As a result, one company moved its headquarters to another city.
- [ ] b. Since they can get low prices, tourists often visit this city.
- [ ] c. Therefore, no one bargains in Canada.

9  Choose the sentence which most likely follows this one: *When people are tired, they are likely to buy less.*
- [ ] a. Consequently, people typically do not buy new beds very often.
- [ ] b. One reason is that people need more than eight hours of sleep.
- [ ] c. Therefore, many companies advertise on TV during the day instead of at night.

10  Choose the sentence which most likely follows this one: *People who care about the planet usually do not buy things that contain many chemicals.*
- [ ] a. For this reason, they avoid buying cleaning products that harm the environment.
- [ ] b. They spend a great deal of money on cleaning products because of the power of advertising.
- [ ] c. As a result, companies try to reduce the number of chemicals in their products.

# Simple Strategies for Making Writing More Academic

## CONNECTING TO THE THEME

**Is social responsibility important to you?**

Consumers should only purchase products from companies that are environmentally friendly.
   **A** Yes, I agree.
   **B** No, I disagree.

Consumers should stop buying one of their favorite products if they discover that children are involved in the production process.
   **A** Yes, immediately.
   **B** No, they should not have to do this.

Consumers should be prepared to pay more for a product from a socially responsible company.
   **A** Yes, the extra cost is justified.
   **B** No, consumers should pay the lowest price they can.

*Mostly As: social responsibility is important to you. Mostly Bs: you might like to find out more about how companies and people can be socially responsible.*

## A. Skill Presentation

The kind of writing that is typically done in school is called **academic writing**. It is different from the writing done outside of school in at least two ways. It is generally more formal and more impersonal.

One way to make writing more academic is to avoid contractions and abbreviations. For example, write *it is* and *do not* rather than *it's* and *don't*. Write out months and city names rather than using abbreviations.

Another simple way to make writing more academic is to avoid using informal expressions like *awesome*, *cash*, or *guys*. Instead, use more formal terms like *impressive*, *money*, or *individuals*.

Finally, avoid the pronoun *you*. Academic writing is impersonal, so the writing should not address the reader directly. For example, instead of writing *you can contribute*, use a general noun like *people* or a more specific noun like *investors*. Then use the pronoun *they* to refer back to these nouns.

Look at these examples.

   **INFORMAL:** You can contribute cash to socially responsible businesses in NY. You'll help protect these businesses by providing funding.

   **ACADEMIC: Investors** can contribute **money** to socially responsible businesses in **New York. They will** help protect these businesses by providing funding.

# B. Over to You

**1** Read the sentences and decide if they are examples of informal or more academic writing. Write *I* for Informal or *A* for Academic.

___ **1** If you disagree with an organization's business practices, you should voice your opinion.

___ **2** The community was wowed by the corporation's new green building.

___ **3** It is not ethical to charge high prices for poor-quality goods.

**2** Read each sentence in the chart, and decide if it is more academic or more informal. Check (✓) the box in the correct column.

| | MORE ACADEMIC | MORE INFORMAL |
|---|---|---|
| 1. Impact Environment manufactures environmentally friendly cleaning products. | | |
| 2. The company's products don't contain chlorine. | | |
| 3. Some studies have shown that chlorine can mess up your respiratory system. | | |
| 4. The company's paper products are made from 100 percent recycled materials. | | |
| 5. Impact Environment works w/ nine other socially responsible organizations. | | |
| 6. One of these organizations is called With the Birches. | | |
| 7. With the Birches has been successful because it's focused on providing environmentally safe paper products at affordable prices. | | |
| 8. Impact Environment requires its employees to evaluate the effect of their own behavior on the planet. | | |
| 9. The guy who started Impact Environment is named Johnny Frieslander. | | |
| 10. Frieslander has said that he'll continue to promote corporate social responsibility. | | |

## CHECK!

Academic writing is more formal and impersonal. To make writing more formal:

**1** avoid contractions and _____.

**2** use _____ instead of the pronoun *you*.

**3** avoid _____ expressions.

# C. Practice

**1 Circle the words that give each sentence a more academic tone.**

1 The reaction to our company's decision to build a green building has been *awesome* | *remarkable*.

2 We have chosen to spend our *funds* | *cash* on social issues rather than advertising.

3 Our executives met with some *politicians* | *guys* from the city government to discuss ways to help the community.

4 City businesses have recently donated large quantities of *equipment* | *stuff* to local schools.

5 The organization has made *a bad* | *an unsatisfactory* attempt to help the community.

6 The organizations *cut a deal* | *reached an agreement* for less expensive manufacturing.

7 The investors are *excited* | *psyched* about this quarter's profits.

8 Competitors *got upset* | *freaked out* when they learned that our profits rose 40 percent after we promised to donate 20 percent of our earnings to charity.

**2 Read each sentence and check (✓) those that are more academic. For the less academic sentences, identify the problem and write *C* for Contraction, *A* for Abbreviation, *PP* for Personal Pronoun, or *IE* for Informal Expression.**

☐ 1 A recent study has shown that during a poor economy, consumers prefer to do business with ethical companies. ___

☐ 2 According to the research, 75 percent of consumers think social responsibility's important. ___

☐ 3 About half of 18- to 35-year-olds are willing to take a lower salary in order to work for a socially responsible company. ___

☐ 4 The clothing manufacturing industry is often viewed as more socially responsible than others, incl. the finance and automotive industries. ___

☐ 5 Approximately 28 percent of consumers will pay ten bucks more for products made using socially responsible practices. ___

☐ 6 Many consumers prefer to buy stuff from a company that supports a specific charity. ___

☐ 7 Back in the day, the clothing industry was not considered socially responsible. ___

☐ 8 Research has also found that 70 percent of people are willing to pay more for products from socially responsible companies. ___

☐ 9 You are more likely to buy from a company that demonstrates social responsibility. ___

☐ 10 Social responsibility isn't important only to consumers; it's also important to employees. ___

## D. Skill Quiz

**Check (✓) the correct answer for each item.**

1 Academic writing is
- ☐ a. used primarily in personal e-mails.
- ☐ b. usually used in school.
- ☐ c. required for most communication.

2 One way to give an academic tone is to
- ☐ a. avoid using pronouns.
- ☐ b. avoid using specific nouns.
- ☐ c. avoid using the pronoun *you*.

3 Another way to give writing a more academic tone is to avoid using
- ☐ a. abbreviations and contractions.
- ☐ b. proper nouns and descriptive adjectives.
- ☐ c. prepositional phrases and time clauses.

4 Another way to give writing a more academic tone is to
- ☐ a. use informal expressions.
- ☐ b. do not give specific examples.
- ☐ c. avoid informal expressions.

5 Which sentence has the most academic tone?
- ☐ a. The founder of a well-known company is not concerned with business growth.
- ☐ b. The founder of a well-known company isn't concerned with business growth.
- ☐ c. The guy who founded a well-known company is not concerned with business growth.

6 Which sentence has the most academic tone?
- ☐ a. The company has donated over $25 mill. to charity.
- ☐ b. The company has donated over $25 million to charity.
- ☐ c. The company's donated over $25 million to charity.

7 Which sentence has the most academic tone?
- ☐ a. If you are a customer of this company, you can decide which charity will receive money.
- ☐ b. The company's customers can decide which charity will receive money.
- ☐ c. People who buy the company's stuff can decide which charity will receive money.

8 What was replaced to make Sentence B more academic?
A: *Customers are totally psyched to buy products from responsible companies.*
B: *Customers are enthusiastic about buying products from responsible companies.*
- ☐ a. the pronoun *you*
- ☐ b. an informal expression
- ☐ c. an abbreviation

9 What was replaced to make Sentence B more academic?
A: *Some people will pay much more to live in an environmentally friendly apt.*
B: *Some people will pay much more to live in an environmentally friendly apartment.*
- ☐ a. an informal expression
- ☐ b. an abbreviation
- ☐ c. a contraction

10 What was replaced to make Sentence B more academic?
A: *Many employees wouldn't mind accepting a lower salary to work for a socially responsible organization.*
B: *Many employees would not mind accepting a lower salary to work for a socially responsible organization.*
- ☐ a. a contraction
- ☐ b. an abbreviation
- ☐ c. an informal expression

ALTERNATIVE ENERGY SOURCES

## CONNECTING TO THE THEME

How much do you know about alternative energy sources? Are these statements true or false?

**1** A wind power converter can create enough electricity to meet the demands of nearly 100 homes.

**2** In 1864, a hotel in Oregon heated rooms using energy from underground hot springs.

**3** Enough sunlight falls on Earth's surface every day to meet global energy demand for one year.

1 False (a wind power converter can create enough electricity to power over 300 homes), 2 True, 3 False (the sunlight that falls on Earth's surface every hour would meet global demand for one year).

# A. Skill Presentation

Plagiarism is when you take another writer's words and present them as your own. Plagiarism is not acceptable, and students who plagiarize can face serious consequences. One effective technique to help avoid plagiarism is **paraphrasing**.

Paraphrasing allows you to incorporate another writer's ideas in your own writing. Here are some tips to help you paraphrase.

- Substitute synonyms for key words and phrases.
- Change the order of the words in a piece of writing you are paraphrasing.
- Do not include new information and do not leave out information.

Read this original sentence and a possible paraphrase.

**ORIGINAL:** Human body heat is an **inexpensive** and **renewable** energy source.

**PARAPHRASE:** One **cheap** and **replaceable** energy source is heat from the human body.

The original words *inexpensive* and *renewable* have been replaced by the synonyms *cheap* and *replaceable*. Note that the word order is also different in the paraphrase; however, the overall meaning of the original sentence has not changed. There is no new information, and no information is missing.

When you paraphrase, remember to include a citation, or details about where you found the ideas. Be sure to use the citation style approved by your teacher.

# B. Over to You

**1** **Read the original sentence and a possible paraphrase. Look at the changes the writer has made, and answer the questions below.**

**Original:** These pipes transfer excess body heat from one building to another.

**Paraphrase:** Additional body heat is moved from building to building by these pipes.

  **1** Which synonyms has the writer used for *transfer* and *excess*? _____ _____

  **2** Which words in the original sentence has the writer replaced with *from building to building*?

        _____

**2** **Read the paragraph. Which of these words and phrases could be used as synonyms to paraphrase the underlined words?**

An [1]<u>inexpensive</u> and [2]<u>renewable</u> source of energy is wind [3]<u>power</u>. It is an [4]<u>excellent</u> [5]<u>alternative</u> to [6]<u>fossil fuels</u>. It is [7]<u>clean</u> and will not [8]<u>harm</u> [9]<u>our planet</u>.

| Earth | energy | very good | fuels like gas and oil | cheap | negatively impact |
|---|---|---|---|---|---|

substitute     will continue to be available     won't produce pollution

  **1** _____

  **2** _____

  **3** _____

  **4** _____

  **5** _____

  **6** _____

  **7** _____

  **8** _____

  **9** _____

## CHECK!

Paraphrasing is an effective technique to avoid plagiarism. To paraphrase:

**1** use _____ in place of key words.

**2** change the _____ of the words in a sentence.

**3** do not include new _____ or leave out _____.

# C. Practice

**1** Read the original sentences and paraphrases, and decide if the paraphrases are acceptable or unacceptable. Write *A* for Acceptable or *U* for Unacceptable.

**1 Original:** In 1860, wood was the main fuel used for heating homes in the United States.
___ **Paraphrase:** Wood was the primary fuel used for warming houses in the United States in 1860.

**2 Original:** By 1950, most buildings and homes were heated by natural gas or electricity.
___ **Paraphrase:** In the 1900s, every house used natural gas for heat, electricity, and light.

**3 Original:** Renewable energy comes from sources in nature like wind, sunlight, and water.
___ **Paraphrase:** Natural sources, such as wind, sun, and water, provide reusable energy.

**4 Original:** People who live near wind farms may be bothered by the noise.
___ **Paraphrase:** The noise from wind farms causes people to move to new locations.

**5 Original:** Solar power changes sunlight into electricity.
___ **Paraphrase:** Solar energy converts light from the sun into electricity.

**6 Original:** Solar power is often used to heat backyard pools.
___ **Paraphrase:** Backyard pools can be too cold to use without proper heat.

**2** Read the original sentences and check (✓) the best paraphrase.

**1** "EV" is the abbreviation for "electric vehicle."

&#9633; a. A shorter way to write or say "electric vehicle" is "EV."
&#9633; b. Electric vehicles can be called "EV" in certain situations.

**2** Energy comes from the sun as both light and heat.

&#9633; a. The sun provides power in the forms of both warmth and light.
&#9633; b. Sunlight is a good alternative energy source and is also renewable.

**3** Riding a bike is one way to avoid contributing to pollution, and it can be healthy.

&#9633; a. One way to avoid polluting the air is to ride a bike, and it may also help improve a person's health.
&#9633; b. Bike riding is better than driving a car because it is a healthy way to lose weight.

**4** The use of renewable energy is becoming more common worldwide.

&#9633; a. More countries are using renewable energy, but there is still not enough global participation.
&#9633; b. All around the world, it is increasingly common to use energy that is renewable.

**5** Water is a frequently used resource that provides energy to 28 million people.

&#9633; a. Water is often used as a source of energy and gives power to almost 30 million consumers.
&#9633; b. People do not appreciate water as an energy source because so many consumers use it.

# D. Skill Quiz

**Check (✓) the correct answer for each item.**

1 Which statement is true?

☐ a. Plagiarism is an effective writing technique.

☐ b. Students who plagiarize will likely face serious consequences.

☐ c. Plagiarism is using relevant information from outside sources.

2 What does a paraphrase let writers do?

☐ a. incorporate other writers' ideas in their own writing

☐ b. plagiarize without breaking rules

☐ c. copy someone else's sentences

3 Which tip can help a writer paraphrase?

☐ a. Memorize the original sentence.

☐ b. Replace words from the original sentence with synonyms.

☐ c. Never change the word order of the original sentence.

4 An acceptable paraphrase

☐ a. should change the meaning of the original sentence significantly.

☐ b. should add interesting information to the original sentence.

☐ c. should not change the overall meaning of the original sentence.

5 *Solar energy is an <u>excellent alternative</u> energy source.*
Which of these could best replace the underlined words?

☐ a. very good substitute

☐ b. not very feasible

☐ c. good, but rarely available

6 *Human body heat is <u>cheap and readily available</u>.*
Which of these could best replace the underlined words?

☐ a. free and ready to use

☐ b. not expensive and simple to use

☐ c. inexpensive and easy to obtain

7 *Electric vehicles are faster than many people may think.*
Which of these is an acceptable paraphrase for this sentence?

☐ a. Electric vehicles are faster than many people think.

☐ b. The majority of people may not realize how fast electric cars are.

☐ c. People think that cars with gasoline engines are faster than electric vehicles.

8 *The sun gives our planet heat and light.*
Which of these is an acceptable paraphrase for this sentence?

☐ a. The Earth receives both light and warmth from the sun.

☐ b. Our planet is warmed by the sun.

☐ c. Sunlight is important to the Earth for two reasons.

9 *The United States receives imported oil from Canada and Mexico.*
Which of these is an acceptable paraphrase for this sentence?

☐ a. Canada imports oil from the United States and Mexico.

☐ b. Imported oil comes from only two countries.

☐ c. Canada and Mexico provide oil to the United States.

10 *One of the problems with fossil fuels is that they are not renewable.*
Which of these is an acceptable paraphrase for this sentence?

☐ a. An issue with fuels like oil and coal is that they will not always be available.

☐ b. One of the problems with fossil fuels is that they are not renewable.

☐ c. Fossil fuels will have to be replaced with alternative fuels because they will not always be available.

# 5

## Topic, Supporting, and Concluding Sentences

**FAMILY SIZE AND PERSONALITY**

## A. Skill Presentation

A good paragraph has a clear topic sentence, relevant supporting sentences, and a strong concluding sentence.

The **topic sentence** is usually the first sentence in the paragraph. It is about one idea (the main idea), but it is fairly broad so it can be expanded on in the rest of the paragraph. It helps the reader understand what the paragraph will be about, but it does not usually include specific examples or details.

**Supporting sentences** follow the topic sentence and support the main idea. They relate only to the topic of the paragraph. They can also give examples and explanations and may provide facts and details about the topic of the paragraph.

A **concluding sentence** ends a paragraph. It restates the main idea of the paragraph and gives the reader something to think about.

For example, read this paragraph about family size.

> [1]The size of an average family varies across countries. [2]For example, in the United States, the average family size is 3.19. [3]That means that there are, on average, about three people per family in the United States. [4]It is possible that differences in family sizes from one country to another influence people's personalities.

The topic sentence (1) in the paragraph above is about family size across countries. The first supporting sentence (2) offers an example of the topic sentence, and the second supporting sentence (3) explains the example. The concluding sentence (4) restates the idea that family size varies depending on the country. In addition, it gives the reader something to think about by mentioning a possible effect of differing family sizes.

# B. Over to You

**1**  **Read the supporting sentences from a paragraph about sibling rivalry, and answer the questions.**

This is often referred to as sibling rivalry. Siblings normally want to receive an equal amount of attention from their parents. If children feel their siblings get more attention, they may get angry.

**1**  Which topic sentence is the most appropriate for this paragraph?

☐  a. Sometimes children compete for their parents' attention.
☐  b. Eighty-two percent of people in the United States have siblings.

**2**  Which concluding sentence is the most appropriate for this paragraph?

☐  a. Another common problem among siblings is a large gap in ages.
☐  b. Although sibling rivalry is very common, it can have negative consequences.

**2**  **Match the topic sentences (1–5) with the appropriate supporting sentences (a–e).**

____ **1**  Firstborn children often have an advantage in life.

____ **2**  Experts say that some children suffer from "middle-child syndrome."

____ **3**  The majority of people in the United States have siblings.

____ **4**  There are many stereotypes about only children.

____ **5**  Older siblings often assume responsibility for their younger siblings.

**a**  In fact, experts estimate that just 18 percent of people are only children.

**b**  For example, studies show that they sometimes have more successful careers than their younger siblings.

**c**  They feel their parents pay more attention to their younger and older siblings than to them.

**d**  They look after them when their parents are busy or unavailable.

**e**  For example, some people think that children without siblings are not comfortable socializing with other children.

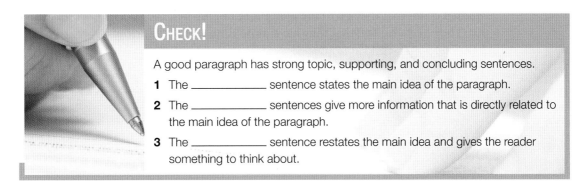

## Check!

A good paragraph has strong topic, supporting, and concluding sentences.

**1**  The _____ sentence states the main idea of the paragraph.

**2**  The _____ sentences give more information that is directly related to the main idea of the paragraph.

**3**  The _____ sentence restates the main idea and gives the reader something to think about.

# C. Practice

**1  Read the paragraphs (1–3) and choose the best topic sentence (a–c) for each one.**

1  ___ This can be due to a variety of circumstances, such as changing environments or large age gaps between siblings. Distinct individual personalities are an important factor in interactions within the family.

2  ___ Older children can help their younger siblings with a variety of everyday tasks. For example, they can help them get dressed or assist them with their homework. Older children help give their siblings the attention they need.

3  ___ They can also give each child plenty of attention and space. Parents should have a clear strategy for dealing with sibling rivalry.

a  It is common for firstborn children to assume some responsibility for their siblings' needs.

b  Despite the fact that siblings share genes, they often have very different personalities.

c  Parents can handle sibling rivalry in a variety of ways. They can focus on family teamwork.

**2  Read the paragraphs (1–3) and choose the best concluding sentence (a–c) for each one.**

1  Some parents believe that a large age gap between siblings gives them more quality time with each child. For example, when the youngest child is born, the firstborn might already be in school. The parents can manage their time and focus on the needs of each child separately. ___

2  Parents who have more than one child often decide how big a gap there should be between siblings. According to some parents, having three or more years between children is beneficial. They say children over the age of three or four are less likely to be jealous when a new sibling is born. On the other hand, other parents argue that a smaller age gap between siblings is better. These parents think it is easier to get the difficult years of parenting young children out of the way at one time. ___

3  Some mothers prefer to have a large age gap between siblings for health reasons. Many women claim that they go to the gym more often when they only have one baby to care for. They may also feel that they have more time to cook nutritious meals when they only have one young child at home. ___

a  Clearly, there is no "right" age gap between siblings, and parents must decide what works best for their family.

b  A large age gap between siblings may help some women feel healthier.

c  One-on-one time with each child is one good argument for a large age gap between siblings.

# D. Skill Quiz

**Check (✓) the correct answer for each item.**

1 A topic sentence
- ☐ a. introduces the main idea of a paragraph.
- ☐ b. supports the first sentence of a paragraph.
- ☐ c. restates the main idea of a paragraph.

2 A good topic sentence
- ☐ a. is very specific.
- ☐ b. contains several examples and facts.
- ☐ c. is fairly broad.

3 Supporting sentences
- ☐ a. introduce the main idea of a paragraph.
- ☐ b. give more information about the topic of a paragraph.
- ☐ c. come at the end of a paragraph.

4 Good supporting sentences
- ☐ a. give broad, general ideas.
- ☐ b. are related to specific ideas in other paragraphs.
- ☐ c. give specific facts, details, and examples.

5 A concluding sentence
- ☐ a. usually comes at the very end of a paragraph.
- ☐ b. is exactly the same as the topic sentence.
- ☐ c. introduces the main idea of the paragraph.

6 A good concluding sentence
- ☐ a. restates the previous supporting sentence.
- ☐ b. restates the main idea of the paragraph.
- ☐ c. introduces a new, unrelated topic.

7 Which is the best topic sentence for a paragraph about how changes within a family affect people's behavior?
- ☐ a. Firstborn children often experience career success later.
- ☐ b. Changing family dynamics contribute to different personalities in a family.
- ☐ c. Some children move several times during their childhood.

8 What is the best topic sentence for a paragraph about how adult siblings behave when they are together?
- ☐ a. The age gap between the two siblings was seven years.
- ☐ b. Many people go back to childhood roles when they are with their family.
- ☐ c. Firstborn children often assume responsibility for their siblings.

9 *Children with no siblings have unique benefits.*
Which supporting sentence does NOT support this topic sentence?
- ☐ a. They have more one-on-one time with their parents.
- ☐ b. They may have more opportunities because their parents have more time and money to spend on them.
- ☐ c. There are many negative stereotypes about them although they usually get along with adults.

10 What is the best concluding sentence for a paragraph about benefits that children with no siblings may experience?
- ☐ a. Being an only child has several advantages.
- ☐ b. Firstborn children are more responsible than only children.
- ☐ c. Only children do not worry as much about sibling rivalry.

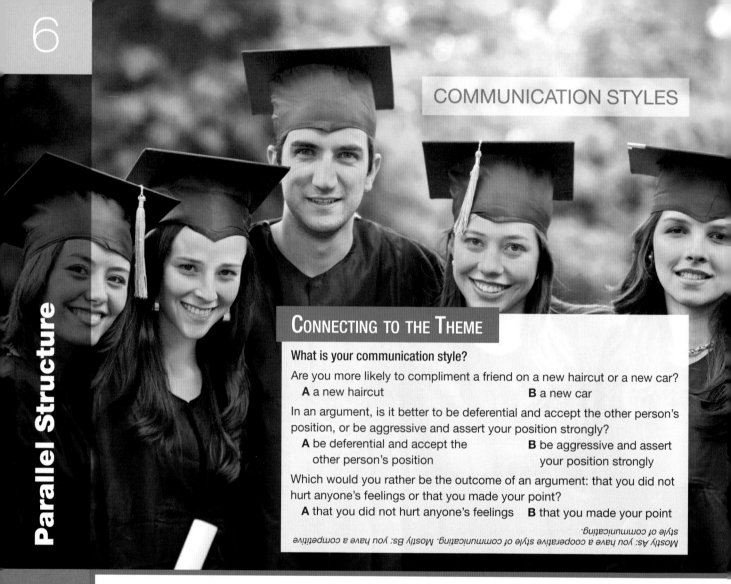

## COMMUNICATION STYLES

**Parallel Structure**

### CONNECTING TO THE THEME

**What is your communication style?**

Are you more likely to compliment a friend on a new haircut or a new car?

**A** a new haircut        **B** a new car

In an argument, is it better to be deferential and accept the other person's position, or be aggressive and assert your position strongly?

**A** be deferential and accept the other person's position      **B** be aggressive and assert your position strongly

Which would you rather be the outcome of an argument: that you did not hurt anyone's feelings or that you made your point?

**A** that you did not hurt anyone's feelings    **B** that you made your point

*Mostly As: you have a cooperative style of communicating. Mostly Bs: you have a competitive style of communicating.*

## A. Skill Presentation

**Parallel structure** means using similar patterns when you write. It helps your sentences flow well, and it makes your writing clearer. Sentences that do not have parallel structure can sound awkward and may be incorrect.

Use parallel structure in lists of words (like nouns, verbs, or adjectives), in lists of phrases, and in lists of clauses. Use parallel structure in comparisons, as well.

Women tend to give similar compliments whether they are **American**, **Canadian**, or **British**.
People give compliments **on appearance**, **on possessions**, **on ability**, or **on personality**.
A person may tell someone **that her hair looks nice**, **that she drives a nice car**, or **that she is kind**. (same verb tenses in clauses)
**Men** do not **compliment each other** as often as **women compliment each other**. (same structure + same verb tenses)

When you write, check your sentences carefully to be sure they have parallel structure. Look for conjunctions like *and*, *or*, and *nor*. They can indicate a list, which needs to have parallel structure. Also look for comparison words like *as* or *than*. Make sure the structure of the things being compared is parallel.

# B. Over to You

**1** The sentences below do not have parallel structure. Correct them in the way suggested.

**1** Some women do not want to be thought of as too assertive or behaving aggressively.

(list of adjectives): _____

**2** Men tended to compliment women more than women were complimenting men.

(same verb tenses): _____

**3** Women give each other compliments to build relationships with friends, relationships with coworkers, and with bosses.

(list of phrases starting with *with*): _____

**2** Read the sentences and pay attention to the words in bold. Do the sentences have parallel structure? Write *Y* for Yes, or *N* for No.

____ **1** When traveling to another country, it is helpful to understand how men and women communicate with **friends**, **family members**, and **co-workers**.

____ **2** Both men and women in China are more likely to respond to a compliment **by giving another compliment** than **by saying thank you**.

____ **3** Not understanding how men and women communicate can lead to **misunderstandings**, **miscommunication**, and **causing other problems**.

____ **4** Some students may get more attention in class because they **raise their hands frequently**, **enjoy speaking in front of others**, and **demonstrate greater confidence**.

____ **5** Women **who feel comfortable speaking** may get the same amount of attention in the classroom as men **who may be acting competitively**.

____ **6** Some researchers believe that girls learn better at all-girls schools because the schools may help improve **cooperation**, **focus**, and **girls feeling good about themselves**.

____ **7** **Getting a higher salary** may be more difficult for some women than **getting an advanced degree**.

____ **8** At many colleges, few women major in **engineering**, **computer science**, or **earn a degree in psychology**.

____ **9** Jobs **offering flexible schedules** and **to help people** may be appealing to some women.

____ **10** Some women believe success at work is possible **with less shy behavior**, **acting more confidently**, and **by speaking more assertively**.

---

**CHECK!**

**1** When you write, make sure your sentences have parallel structure. Use _____ word patterns in lists of words, phrases, or clauses.

**2** Sentences that express _____ must have parallel structure, as well. Parallel structure makes your sentences flow well, and it makes your writing clearer.

# C. Practice

**1**  **Read the paragraph and underline the sentences that do not have parallel structure. How many are there?**

¹Research shows that communication, language, and gestures are sometimes used differently by men and women. ²Men's language is often direct, honest, and contains facts. ³Women's language is sometimes not as direct as men's language. ⁴Women often use language that is indirect, that is deferential, and their language is nurturing. ⁵Research shows that many women like to discuss relationships, about how they feel, and personal experiences. ⁶Many men avoid discussion of personal issues. ⁷Men typically use language to exchange information or to solve problems. ⁸One way of communicating is not necessarily better than the other way people communicate.

There are _____ sentences without parallel structure. Sentences: _____

**2**  **Circle the words that give each sentence parallel structure.**

**1**  Research shows that men and women use language differently when they give compliments and *that arguments happen | when they have arguments | if they argue with each other.*

**2**  Women often want to discuss, debate, and *solve | finding solutions to | trying to solve* relationship problems.

**3**  Men tend to avoid discussing problems or *about their feelings | how they feel | feelings.*

**4**  Some women think that men rarely listen, that they hardly ever answer questions, and *have to be correct | that they never admit mistakes | could have been better listeners.*

**5**  Some say younger men talk about their feelings more than older men *talk about their feelings | discuss how they feel | with their feelings.*

**6**  Some people cry to stop an argument, *getting what they want, | to get what they want, | it can help them get what they want,* or to avoid problems.

**7**  When men argue, they can be defensive, *with aggression, | who may act aggressively, | aggressive,* and angry.

**8**  When women argue, men may sometimes interpret their words and actions as confusing, emotional, or *indirect | being indirect | can be indirect.*

**9**  Some *individual psychologist | psychologists | who study psychology* and language experts disagree; they do not believe that the way men and women use language to argue is that different.

**10**  It is believed that that cultural differences are more significant than *arguing differently | gender differences | when people argue.*

# D. Skill Quiz

**Check (✓) the correct answer for each item.**

1  What is parallel structure?
- [ ] a. relating sentences to the topic
- [ ] b. using similar word patterns
- [ ] c. comparing two or more things

2  Use parallel structure
- [ ] a. with multiple subjects.
- [ ] b. in run-on sentences.
- [ ] c. in lists and comparisons.

3  Which words can help you identify sentences that need to have parallel structure?
- [ ] a. subjects and verbs
- [ ] b. conjunctions in lists and comparison words
- [ ] c. objects and prepositions

4  Which sentence has parallel structure?
- [ ] a. Adults, teenagers, and children communicate differently.
- [ ] b. Adults, teenagers, and those who are young communicate differently.
- [ ] c. People who are older, when people are teenagers, and children communicate differently.

5  Which sentence has parallel structure?
- [ ] a. Teenage girls often communicate through notes and through text messages.
- [ ] b. Teenage girls often communicate through notes and sending text messages.
- [ ] c. Teenage girls often communicate by writing notes and to send text messages.

6  Which sentence has parallel structure?
- [ ] a. Teenage boys communicate differently than girls who are teens.
- [ ] b. Teenage boys communicate differently than teenage girls.
- [ ] c. Teenage boys communicate differently talking to girls.

7  *Girls often develop language skills sooner ___.*
Choose the option that gives this sentence parallel structure.
- [ ] a. than boys develop slowly
- [ ] b. that boys
- [ ] c. than boys

8  *In girls, the part of the brain that controls expression, verbal skill, and ___ develops earlier.*
Choose the option that gives this sentence parallel structure.
- [ ] a. that is in control of social behavior
- [ ] b. social behavior
- [ ] c. to control social behavior

9  *Research shows that girls use the abstract part of the brain when processing language verbally or ___.*
Choose the option that gives this sentence parallel structure.
- [ ] a. with visibility
- [ ] b. vision
- [ ] c. visually

10  *Gender studies is a field that is <u>complicated, that is complex, and that is interesting</u>.*
Which words can be removed from the underlined part of this sentence?
- [ ] a. and, that
- [ ] b. that, is
- [ ] c. complex, interesting

FAMILY VALUES IN DIFFERENT CULTURES

## CONNECTING TO THE THEME

If you were to write an essay on family values in current times, which of the following sources would be appropriate?

**A** a recent article by Professor Patrick J. DiVietri, Ph.D. of the Family Life Institute

**B** your friend's personal blog about her family life

**C** an encyclopedia that is 30 years old

*A: it is current and was written by a qualified expert in the field.*

## A. Skill Presentation

When you write an academic essay, it is important to use appropriate sources. Appropriate sources are factual and accurate. Appropriate information will make your writing stronger.

**Appropriate sources** include reference books like dictionaries and encyclopedias, newspapers, academic journals, and books by experts in the field you are writing about. In addition, some magazine articles and articles on websites may also be appropriate.

Before you use any sources, always:
- check the date. Use sources that have been published as recently as possible.
- check the author. The author should be an expert in the field you are writing about (especially for Internet articles).
- check the writing for facts. Look for statistics, documented research, and quotations from other experts. Avoid writing that includes opinions unsupported with facts.
- check the writing style. Avoid sources that contain a lot of grammar or spelling mistakes.

Look at this list of sources one writer researched for an essay about family values today and in the past.

1  a dictionary to define *family values*  ✓
2  a journal article by a psychologist about how family values have changed in the past 100 years  ✓
3  a newspaper article from 1950 about family life  ✓
4  a magazine article about music today and in the past  ✗
5  a blog by a classmate who thinks his life was better in the past  ✗

Numbers 1, 2, and 3 are all appropriate sources of information. The dictionary is a good source for defining a term like *family values*. The journal article is relevant and was written by an expert. The newspaper article is also relevant; it describes family life in the past. Numbers 4 and 5 are inappropriate sources of information because the magazine is not related to the topic, and the blog contains personal opinion and is not written by an expert.

# B. Over to You

**1** Read the essay topic and the following list of sources a writer has researched. Check (✓) the two sources that are appropriate for the topic, and decide why the other two are inappropriate.

**Essay Topic:** Predictions for What Family Values Will Be Like in 2050

☐ **1** a book by a sociology researcher about family values published in 1900

☐ **2** a journal article by a scientist explaining how technology will change family values in this century

☐ **3** an interview with a psychologist about her research on family values and the future

☐ **4** a blog by a 12-year-old about her predictions for life in the future

Source ___ is inappropriate because _____.

Source ___ is inappropriate because _____.

**2** Read the essay topic and the descriptions of sources in the chart. Decide if each source is appropriate or not, and check (✓) the box in the correct column.

**Essay Topic:** How Television Changed Family Life Over Time

| | APPROPRIATE | NOT APPROPRIATE |
|---|---|---|
| 1. an encyclopedia that explains the history of the invention of television | | |
| 2. a blog by a 16-year-old about his family's TV watching habits | | |
| 3. an academic journal article by a historian about the effects of TV on family norms | | |
| 4. an article on a Canadian government website that includes statistics about TV viewing habits from 1950 to 2012 | | |
| 5. a magazine article about which TV programs celebrities watch | | |
| 6. a book that describes a study comparing families' TV viewing habits now with viewing habits in the 1960s | | |
| 7. your mother's ideas about which TV shows are good for families to watch together | | |
| 8. a journal article written in 1920 about technology that might be used to create television | | |

## CHECK!

**1** Appropriate sources are factual and _____. Information from these sources will make your writing _____.

**2** Sources that contain _____ that are not supported with facts, and sources that are not written by an _____ in the field, are inappropriate.

# C. Practice

**1** Read essay topics 1 and 2 and the list of sources (a–f), and decide which two sources are appropriate for each essay topic. There are two sources that will not be used.

1 Family Life in the 1800s ___ ___          2 Life in a Modern Family ___ ___

a  an excerpt from a scientific journal about family life more than 150 years ago

b  an interview with a grandparent about growing up in a large family in Iowa in the 1950s

c  a journal article about modern inventions that make family life easier

d  an article from a parenting magazine about typical families in today's world

e  a book about nineteenth-century families by a well-known historian

f  a magazine article describing a TV show that sends people to live with different families

**2** Read the paragraphs from two students' essays on television and family values. Underline the sources, decide if each one is appropriate or inappropriate, and choose a reason why. More than one reason may apply.

### Student 1

Most families can make watching television work with their values. Not all TV shows fit with everyone's values. For example, some shows are extremely violent. Maria Brooks, movie reviewer in *What You Want to Know* magazine, says that many parents get upset when their children watch violent shows on TV. In her opinion, children will behave better if they avoid watching shows with unsuitable content. In an article in our college's newspaper from January 1987, engineering student David Consuelo writes that parents should always watch TV with their children. Then they can discuss what happens in the shows. For example, local parent Michael Carter wrote on his blog, "TV can be educational. However, I always wotch with my children so's I can make sure what they seeing is apropriate."

### Student 2

Most parents can make watching television work with their family values. However, there are shows on TV that are inconsistent with some people's family values. For example, some TV shows contain violent images, and many parents do not want their children to watch these shows. Dr. Garcia, psychologist and author of *Media and the Family*, recommends in his book that parents restrict their children's television viewing. He recommends avoiding shows about topics that contradict the family's values. Dr. Larson, a psychologist at Peseco State University, suggests in a recent article in the journal *Family Now* that parents should watch TV with their children. They can then discuss the shows and answer their children's questions. Her research shows that a family discussion about TV shows helps children develop their moral sense.

Source 1 _____    Source 2 _____    Source 3 _____    Source 4 _____    Source 5 _____

a  The source is old.

b  The source is not an expert in the field you are writing about (especially for Internet articles).

c  The source includes opinions unsupported by facts.

d  The source contains a lot of grammar or spelling mistakes.

e  The source is current.

f  The source is an expert in the field you are writing about.

g  The source supports opinions with facts.

# D. Skill Quiz

**Check (✓) the correct answer for each item.**

1  Which of these sources are appropriate for an academic essay?

☐ a. blogs and newspapers about recent fashion trends

☐ b. personal experiences and opinions of friends you trust

☐ c. newspapers and reference books

2  When is it appropriate to use a website as a source?

☐ a. when it has information that is more interesting than a book

☐ b. when it contains facts and research written by experts

☐ c. when searching for the website is quick and simple

3  Why is it important to look at the writing style of a source?

☐ a. because you should correct the grammar before you use the source

☐ b. because if it contains errors, it may not be a reliable source

☐ c. because you should make a note in your essay if the original source has errors

4  What are two ways to determine if a source is appropriate?

☐ a. check that the author is an expert, and check that it contains facts

☐ b. check that the facts are supported by opinions, and check that the date is this year

☐ c. check that there are not too many errors, and check that the author has written several other books

5  Which sentence is the most appropriate in an essay about personal values?

☐ a. Most students in this class do not think people should have to tell others what they value.

☐ b. A recent survey shows that 90 percent of college students believe that personal space is important.

☐ c. According to *StarBrite* magazine, singer Maeve Malone demonstrates loyalty to her family members.

6  *People had large families in the 1800s because they needed many people to work on farms in order to survive.*
Which source was probably used for this sentence from an essay?

☐ a. an interview with a parent about life when they were young

☐ b. a dictionary

☐ c. a book about farm life in the 1800s

7  *A value helps you decide what is right or wrong and how to behave in certain situations.*
Which source was probably used for this sentence from an essay?

☐ a. a blog about modern family life

☐ b. a dictionary

☐ c. an academic journal

8  Which sentence is inappropriate for an essay about family values in Brazil?

☐ a. My cousin went to Brazil last year to stay with a family, and she told me about their values.

☐ b. According to Dr. Brito at the Brazil Family Study Center, families offer each other stability.

☐ c. Statistics show the average size of families in Brazil is decreasing.

## CONNECTING TO THE THEME

How much do you know about dressing for work in the United States? Are these statements true or false?

**1** It is not important to learn the dress code, or rules for dressing, when you start a new job.

**2** The dress code in most financial companies is similar to the dress code in most IT companies.

**3** Companies in Los Angeles tend to have formal dress codes, whereas companies in New York tend to have more casual dress codes.

**4** Dark pants are perfectly acceptable if you work in an office. Jeans are also appropriate.

**5** It's not necessary for men to wear both a suit jacket and a necktie for client meetings.

*All are false.*

## A. Skill Presentation

Coherent writing is well organized and has ideas that fit together clearly and smoothly. Connectors can help make a piece of writing more coherent. In a comparison essay, when the writer compares two or more things, connectors can show how they are alike or how they are different.

Some connectors that show how things are alike are *one similarity, another similarity, similarly*, and *likewise*. These words and phrases show similarities between ideas in different sentences. Other useful connectors to show similarities include *similar to, the same as, like, both*, and *also*. These words help link ideas within a sentence.

Read these sentences from a comparison essay that shows similarities between the way people dress in Japan and China. Look at the **connectors** the writer uses to make the writing more coherent. *Similar to* links one idea to a similar one within a single sentence. *One similarity* and *another similarity* introduce new information. *Also* and *likewise* link ideas between sentences.

> The way people dress in Japan is **similar to** the way people dress in China. **One similarity** is the level of formality. Clothing is usually formal in Japan. It is **also** formal in China. **Another similarity** is that women usually do not wear pants to work. Women in Japan often wear skirts and blouses or dresses. **Likewise**, women in China usually wear conservative skirts and blouses to work.

Some connectors that help show how things are different are *one difference, another difference, however*, and *on the other hand*. Other useful connectors to show differences include *instead, instead of, although, but*, and *whereas*.

# B. Over to You

**1  Read the paragraph from a comparison essay. Underline the five connectors the writer has used to show how things are different, and answer the questions below.**

In Malaysia, the clothes people wear for evening business events are different from the clothes usually worn during the workday. One difference is the clothing that men wear. For evening events, they generally wear short-sleeved shirts and pants instead of suits. Another difference is the clothing that women wear. During the day, they normally wear skirts, but in the evening, they tend to wear pants. Clothing during the workday is formal for men and women. However, clothes for evening business events can be casual.

1  Which connectors does the writer use to link ideas within a single sentence?

_____ and _____

2  Which connectors introduce new information?

_____ and _____

3  Which connector links an idea in one sentence to an idea in another sentence?

_____

**2  Read the sentences and circle the connectors. Decide if each connector shows a similarity or a difference, and write *S* for Similarity or *D* for Difference.**

___ 1  Doctors Without Borders is a global organization. Similarly, the Red Cross has offices all over the world.

___ 2  The dress code in Australia is usually formal, whereas the dress code in the United States is often casual.

___ 3  Both American Apparel and H&M have stores all over the world.

___ 4  Many companies communicate with employees primarily through e-mail. Some companies communicate using teleconferences instead of e-mail.

___ 5  Doctors Without Borders, like the Red Cross, helps people around the world.

___ 6  People usually wear formal clothing to work in Mexico City; however, the dress code is sometimes casual in smaller cities.

___ 7  It is not easy to start a global company. It can also be difficult to start a small local company.

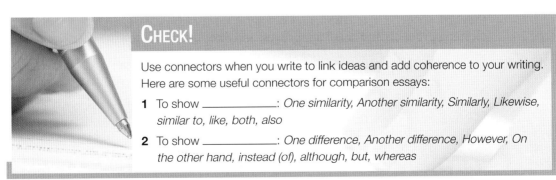

## Check!

Use connectors when you write to link ideas and add coherence to your writing. Here are some useful connectors for comparison essays:

1  To show _____: *One similarity, Another similarity, Similarly, Likewise, similar to, like, both, also*

2  To show _____: *One difference, Another difference, However, On the other hand, instead (of), although, but, whereas*

# C. Practice

**1** **Circle the correct connectors for each item.**

1 There are many ways a global company can use the Internet to communicate. Employees can listen to podcasts on the Internet, *and | but* they can also watch training videos.

2 Teleconferencing is a good way for global companies to communicate. Global companies can *instead | also* use webcasts to communicate.

3 Communicating by e-mail can be impersonal. *On the other hand, | Similarly,* teleconferencing is often a more personal way to communicate.

4 It is easy to create a video podcast that can be shared with the company. *Although | Both* video cameras and computers are needed to create high-quality video podcasts.

5 When a group of businesspeople meet for the first time in Brazil, the meeting is often formal. *Likewise, | However,* meetings that take place later are often informal.

6 Items not on the agenda are often discussed at the end of a meeting. *Although | Whereas* this usually happens, sometimes meetings only address agenda items.

7 Meetings in the United States usually start at the scheduled time. Canada is *similar to | instead of* the United States in this regard.

**2** **Read the paragraph from a comparison essay, and complete it with the connectors below that show difference.**

| another difference | however | one difference | whereas |
|---|---|---|---|

Tesota and Willow are two very different companies. ¹_____ is the dress code. Tesota does not allow its employees to wear jeans, ²_____ Willow employees can wear jeans on Fridays. ³_____ is the number of meetings the companies have. The employees at Tesota have to attend several meetings. ⁴_____, there are very few meetings at Willow. In conclusion, employees at Tesota and Willow work in significantly different environments.

**3** **Read the paragraph from a comparison essay, and complete it with the connectors below that show similarity.**

| another similarity | both | likewise | one similarity |
|---|---|---|---|

JonesMart and ShopLots are similar companies. ¹_____ is the types of products they sell. ²_____ companies sell items for the home. For instance, JonesMart sells cleaning products and small appliances, and ShopLots does, too. ³_____ is the size of the companies. JonesMart has stores in more than 45 states. ⁴_____, ShopLots has stores in more than 40 states. In summary, JonesMart and ShopLots have much in common.

# D. Skill Quiz

**Check (✓) the correct answer for each item.**

1 What do connectors do in an essay?
   - [ ] a. state the topic
   - [ ] b. link ideas
   - [ ] c. fix sentence fragments

2 What does a comparison essay do?
   - [ ] a. shows results or effects of an event
   - [ ] b. gives the reader's opinion on a topic
   - [ ] c. shows how two or more things are alike or different

3 Which connectors show similarities?
   - [ ] a. first, second, finally
   - [ ] b. although, but, on the other hand
   - [ ] c. also, both, likewise

4 Which connectors show differences?
   - [ ] a. whereas, instead, however
   - [ ] b. next, then, in summary
   - [ ] c. both, also, similarly

5 Which sentence shows a similarity?
   - [ ] a. Meetings start on time in the main office, but they never start on time in a few of the overseas offices.
   - [ ] b. Although the meeting usually begins with a financial report, today it started with a sales presentation.
   - [ ] c. The meetings at the office in Taiwan are similar to the meetings at the office in Canada.

6 Which sentence shows a difference?
   - [ ] a. Whereas business clothing can be very casual in the United States, it is usually more formal in Japan.
   - [ ] b. One similarity between businesses in Japan and Malaysia is the way people dress for work.
   - [ ] c. Businessmen wear suits, and businesswomen also wear suits.

7 Which sentence shows a similarity?
   - [ ] a. However, you should first discuss the problem with your manager before replying to the e-mail.
   - [ ] b. Communication problems can happen both in face-to-face communications and in e-mails.
   - [ ] c. Although communication problems happen, they are rare at Tesota.

8 Which sentence shows a difference?
   - [ ] a. People wear jeans on Friday, whereas they must wear suits on other days.
   - [ ] b. Both companies allow employees to wear jeans on Friday.
   - [ ] c. For example, employees can also wear jeans on Friday and on Monday.

9 *Global companies face many problems.* Which sentence most likely follows this one?
   - [ ] a. The sales department is doing well, too.
   - [ ] b. National companies also have significant challenges.
   - [ ] c. In contrast, cultural differences can be a problem.

10 *Many businesspeople communicate with cell phones.* Which sentence most likely follows this one?
   - [ ] a. Similarly, they take public transportation to work.
   - [ ] b. For example, they watch both podcasts and training videos on their office computers.
   - [ ] c. However, they often cannot use their phones when traveling in other countries.

**Sentence Variety**

### CONNECTING TO THE THEME

Former U.S. president Bill Clinton said, "When we make college more affordable, we make the American Dream more achievable." Do you agree that the American Dream is easier to achieve if the cost of college is lower?

**A** Yes, I do. The American Dream is only possible if you go to college.

**B** No, I think you can achieve the American Dream without going to college.

**C** Yes, I agree that it would make the American Dream easier.

## A. Skill Presentation

Good writers use a variety of sentence types to add impact to their writing and to help keep readers interested. There are a number of techniques for adding variety to your sentences.

Don't start every sentence the same way. Look at these sentences from a paragraph about a boy named Freddy Adu. Both begin with time clauses that start with *when*. However, moving the time clause *when he was very young* to the end of the sentence creates variety.

> When he was a boy, Freddy Adu dreamed of being a soccer star. **When he was very young**, he started playing soccer. ✗
> When he was a boy, Freddy Adu dreamed of being a soccer star. He started playing soccer **when he was very young**. ✓

Use different words to convey the same meaning. For example, these sentences both include *$500,000*. Changing *$500,000* to *a half a million dollars* makes the sentences more varied.

> Freddy was offered **$500,000** to play professional soccer. A team in Washington, D.C., offered him $500,000 in 2003.
> Freddy was offered **a half a million dollars** to play professional soccer. A team in Washington, D.C., offered him $500,000 in 2003. ✓

Use different sentence types. Use a mix of **simple**, **compound**, and **complex** sentences.

> ᔆFreddy's mother wanted a better life. She entered the visa lottery. ᶜNot many people win this lottery, but the Adu family did. ᶜˣFreddy became a successful soccer player after the family moved to the United States.

# B. Over to You

**1** Read the original sentences and the sentences with more variety. Check (✓) the two techniques the writer uses to add variety to the sentences.

**Original Sentences:** While living in Ghana, Freddy Adu played soccer often. Before moving to the United States, he often played without shoes.

**Sentences with More Variety:** Freddy Adu played soccer every day while living in Ghana. Before moving to the United States, he often played without shoes.

- ☐ a. change the order of phrases and clauses
- ☐ b. use different words to express the same meaning
- ☐ c. change the sentence type

**2** Read the pairs of sentences and decide which technique was used to change the original sentences. Write *NO* for New Order, *DW* for Different Words, or *NST* for New Sentence Type.

**1** A common belief in the United States is that individuals' dreams are achievable if they work hard.

___ **Revised Sentence:** A common belief in the United States is that if individuals work hard, their dreams are achievable.

**2** A sense of optimism can have remarkable effects on people's success during challenging times.

___ **Revised Sentence:** A positive outlook can have remarkable effects on people's success during difficult times.

**3** Ana Soto overcame great challenges in her lifetime, so she was a role model for her children.

___ **Revised Sentence:** Because Ana Soto overcame great challenges in her lifetime, she was a role model for her children.

**4** People typically feel more secure when the economy is strong in their region.

___ **Revised Sentence:** When the economy is strong in their region, people typically feel more secure.

**5** The nurses work very hard, and they are greatly appreciated by their patients as a result.

___ **Revised Sentence:** Working very hard, the nurses are greatly appreciated by their patients.

**6** In contemporary society, the definition of "family" is changing.

___ **Revised Sentence:** In modern society, the meaning of the word "family" is changing.

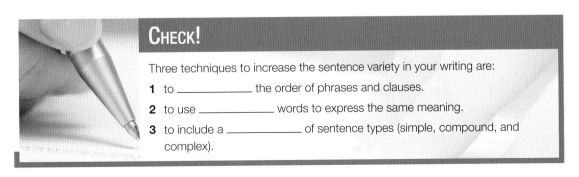

## CHECK!

Three techniques to increase the sentence variety in your writing are:

**1** to _____ the order of phrases and clauses.

**2** to use _____ words to express the same meaning.

**3** to include a _____ of sentence types (simple, compound, and complex).

# C. Practice

**1** Read the paragraph from an essay about the American Dream. For each numbered blank, decide which additional sentence, *A* or *B*, should come next to add the most variety.

The American Dream means different things to different people. It means buying a house for many people. [1]___. For other people, the American Dream has more to do with the type of car they drive. An expensive car is important to them. [2]___. When some people are asked to define the American Dream, they talk about happiness more than physical possessions. [3]___. Quite a few people want to be their own boss, and for them, the American Dream is about owning a business. [4]___. Some people dream about fame. They want to be a famous athlete or a respected actor. The American Dream can have a variety of meanings. In addition, it can be challenging to attain. [5]___.

**1** **A** Buying a house is a goal. Many Americans pursue this goal.
   **B** Home ownership is a goal that a large number of Americans pursue.

**2** **A** When they drive a luxury automobile, they have a feeling of success.
   **B** They may drive a luxury car. They feel successful as a result.

**3** **A** If they try to define the American Dream, they do not talk about material possessions.
   **B** Material possessions are not cited as an important part of the American Dream.

**4** **A** While they like the freedom of working for themselves, they know it can be risky.
   **B** Many people want to be their own boss, but they know it can be risky.

**5** **A** While it is nice to dream, real success comes from hard work.
   **B** Dreams are nice. Working hard is also important.

**2** Match the original sentences (1–6) with the correct alternative sentences (a–f) that would add more variety to a piece of writing.

___ **1** People who live with fewer material possessions tend to more fully appreciate simple pleasures.

___ **2** Having many possessions does not guarantee happiness.

___ **3** It can be difficult for many people to maintain a positive outlook when necessities become more expensive.

___ **4** Some people lose hope during a weak economy. Other people feel that it presents an exciting challenge.

___ **5** Purchasing a home is not for everyone because it usually costs a great deal of money.

___ **6** Working hard does not always ensure that employees will be able to keep their jobs.

**a** As the cost of living rises, it can be hard to have a sense of optimism.

**b** When they own less, people often have a greater appreciation for simplicity.

**c** Employees may work hard, but this will not necessarily increase their job security.

**d** Homeownership can be expensive, so it is not the right choice for every person.

**e** Joy does not necessarily come from owning material objects.

**f** While some feel hopeless during hard economic times, others are inspired.

# D. Skill Quiz

**Check (✓) the correct answer for each item.**

1 Good writers use a variety of sentences
- ☐ a. to add length and complexity.
- ☐ b. to add impact and interest.
- ☐ c. to add additional facts and examples.

2 Which of these is not a technique for adding sentence variety?
- ☐ a. including new information
- ☐ b. using different words to express the same idea
- ☐ c. including different sentence types

3 By using a mix of ___ sentences, writers add variety to their work.
- ☐ a. dependent and independent
- ☐ b. long, medium, and short
- ☐ c. simple, compound, and complex

4 *People think of homeownership when they think of the American Dream.*
Which revision of this sentence uses the technique of moving a phrase or a clause?
- ☐ a. When they think of the American Dream, people think of homeownership.
- ☐ b. People think of owning a home when they think of the American Dream.
- ☐ c. People want to buy a house, but they cannot afford the American Dream of homeownership.

5 *While we were living in poverty, we still felt a sense of optimism about the future.*
Which revision of this sentence uses different words that mean the same thing?
- ☐ a. While we were poor, we continued to feel hopeful.
- ☐ b. We were living in poverty. However, we still felt a sense of optimism.
- ☐ c. We were living in poverty, but we still felt a sense of optimism.

6 *The cost of living continues to rise, and job security is not always achievable.*
Which revision of this sentence uses a different sentence type?
- ☐ a. Prices continue to increase, and not everyone has job security.
- ☐ b. The cost of living continues to rise; in addition, job security is not always achievable.
- ☐ c. Necessary items are becoming more expensive to buy, and people are at risk of losing their jobs.

7 *When he was a young boy, Freddy Adu dreamed of being a soccer player. He did not know that his dream would come true.*
Which option adds the least variety as a continuation of this paragraph?
- ☐ a. Freddy Adu became the youngest professional soccer player in the United States at age 14, and this was considered remarkable.
- ☐ b. Remarkably, Freddy Adu became the youngest professional soccer player in the United States when he was just 14.
- ☐ c. Fourteen-year-old Freddy Adu played professional soccer. He was the youngest player. This accomplishment was remarkable.

8 *Ellen's mother was successful and content. Ellen strived to be more like her.*
Which option adds the most variety as a continuation of this paragraph?
- ☐ a. Because she had a positive role model, Ellen was inspired to achieve her dreams.
- ☐ b. She had a good role model. This inspired her to achieve her dreams.
- ☐ c. Her mother was a positive role model. She provided great inspiration.

IMMIGRANT LIFE

### CONNECTING TO THE THEME

According to Malcolm Wallop, "Many immigrants cherish ... the value of education more than 7th or 8th generation Americans." Do you agree?

**A** Yes, it's easy for 7th or 8th generation Americans to take education for granted.

**B** No, I think everyone realizes how important education is equally.

## A. Skill Presentation

Punctuating direct quotations correctly is an important step in ensuring accuracy in your writing and avoiding plagiarism.

Use double **quotation marks** around quoted text and single quotation marks around quoted text within a direct quotation.

> According to Diego Garcia, "Regardless of their economic status, European immigrants in the nineteenth century were allowed into the United States. This idea is captured in the words 'Give me your tired, your poor' on the Statue of Liberty."

When we use a **reporting phrase**, such as *according to*, *said*, or *explained*, we separate it from the quotation with **commas**. When the reporting phrase follows the quotation, the comma goes at the end of the quotation, inside the quotation marks.

> "There are not as many jobs in the auto industry now," Kate Miller **said,** "but people continue to come to Detroit."

**Periods** and **question marks** go at the end of a quotation, inside the quotation marks.

> Ms. Miller asked, "Because of the decline in the labor market, will fewer immigrants move to Detroit in the future?"

# B. Over to You

**1  Read the sentences. Check (✓) two that use correct punctuation in direct quotations.**

☐  a. In her recent book, Dr. Rhea Mehta states, "Big cities have historically attracted immigrants from many countries."

☐  b. In her recent book, Dr. Rhea Mehta states "Big cities have historically attracted immigrants from many countries."

☐  c. "Big cities have historically attracted immigrants from many countries," Dr. Rhea Mehta states in her recent book.

☐  d. "Big cities have historically attracted immigrants from many countries." Dr. Rhea Mehta states in her recent book.

**2  Read the original sentences and the quotations, and decide if the quotations have been punctuated correctly. Write *C* for Correct or *I* for Incorrect.**

1  **Original:** People from Asia started coming to California during the 1849 Gold Rush.
___ **Quotation:** According to Kate Lyden, "People from Asia started coming to California during the 1849 Gold Rush."

2  **Original:** Many people came from China, Japan, and South Korea.
___ **Quotation:** "Ms. Lyden stated "Many people immigrated from China, Japan, and South Korea."

3  **Original:** As a result of earlier migrations, there are now many Chinese newspapers in California.
___ **Quotation:** "As a result of earlier migrations, sociologist Tim Reynolds claims, there are now many Chinese newspapers in California."

4  **Original:** There are many Japanese immigrants in California, and there are many American-born Japanese people, too.
___ **Quotation:** "There are many Japanese immigrants in California," says Dr. Ito, 'and there are many American-born Japanese people, too.'

5  **Original:** A substantial number of Asian Americans voted for Barack Obama in 2008.
___ **Quotation:** "According to American Sun, 'A substantial number of Asian Americans voted for Barack Obama in 2008.'"

6  **Original:** Many Asians and Asian Americans attend universities in California.
___ **Quotation:** "Many Asians and Asian Americans attend universities in California," says Dr. Hallstead.

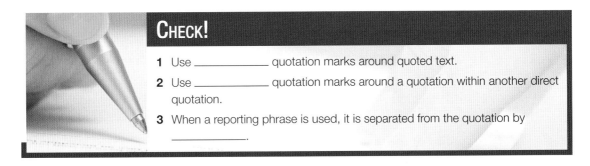

## CHECK!

1  Use _____ quotation marks around quoted text.

2  Use _____ quotation marks around a quotation within another direct quotation.

3  When a reporting phrase is used, it is separated from the quotation by _____.

# C. Practice

**1   These sentences have not been punctuated correctly. Add commas where necessary.**

1   According to *AK* magazine "Many people went to Alaska during the Klondike Gold Rush of 1897."

2   "One hundred thousand people set off for Alaska" Dr. Ben Montgomery said "but only 30,000 made it there."

3   Dr. Laura Byrd states "People in Seattle made large sums of money selling supplies to people heading to Alaska."

4   "Some people traveled to Alaska by boat" reports *AK* magazine "and others traveled on land through Canada."

5   Marty Wendall claims "My great-grandfather was a miner in Alaska, and he always said 'It's rough work.'"

6   "Fairbanks became an important city during the Gold Rush" according to *News Source Alaska*.

7   "People came to Alaska during the Klondike Gold Rush from Canada and England" says Dr. Maria Gomez "as well as from places as far away as South Africa."

8   Museum director Kim Park states "We have a permanent display of mining life on the first floor."

9   According to historian Barbara Hert "Today you can visit old mining towns in many parts of Alaska."

10   "Our ships stop at a mining town established in the 1800s" says Todd Jones of *Cruise Alaska* "and you can explore an abandoned gold mine."

**2   These sentences have not been punctuated correctly. Add double quotation marks where necessary.**

1   According to *Detroit Now*, People started to come to Michigan from the Middle East in the late 1880s.

2   Dr. Mark Hayek says, People from the Middle East originally came to Michigan to work in the Detroit auto industry.

3   At first, the people who came to Michigan were mostly Lebanese, says Dr. Hayek, as well as Syrian.

4   People also immigrated to Michigan from Iraq and Yemen, states Dr. Hayek.

5   *Detroit Now* reports, People continued to immigrate to Michigan even after the auto industry declined.

6   The bulk of the people from the Middle East in Michigan are Lebanese, claims Dr. Hayek, and they live in the Detroit area.

7   Historian Jennifer Owens says, The population of people from the Middle East in the Detroit area grew by over 65 percent from 1990 to 2000.

8   According to one report, the number of people from the Middle East is likely to grow 'by leaps and bounds' in the future, says Ms. Owens.

# D. Skill Quiz

**Check (✓) the correct answer for each item.**

**1** What is a direct quotation?

☐ a. writing that uses the exact wording of the original source

☐ b. information from a source that you must put in your own words

☐ c. an accurate summary of information from a reliable source

**2** What punctuation indicates a quotation from the original text?

☐ a. single quotation marks

☐ b. double quotation marks

☐ c. commas

**3** We use ___ around quoted text within a direct quotation.

☐ a. double quotation marks

☐ b. single quotation marks

☐ c. no quotation marks

**4** In direct quotations, where do periods and question marks go?

☐ a. outside the quotation marks

☐ b. inside the quotation marks

☐ c. before the reporting phrase

**5** When a reporting phrase comes after a direct quotation, the comma goes

☐ a. after the reporting phrase and outside the quotation marks.

☐ b. after the quotation but outside the quotation marks.

☐ c. after the quotation but inside the quotation marks.

**6** Which direct quotation uses a comma correctly?

☐ a. According to *Web Stats*, "Many immigrants first come to big cities."

☐ b. According to *Web Stats* ", Many immigrants first come to big cities."

☐ c. According to *Web Stats* "Many immigrants first come to big cities."

**7** Which direct quotation uses commas correctly?

☐ a. "In the 1800s", reports *Detroit Now*, "many people came to Detroit."

☐ b. "In the 1800s," reports *Detroit Now*, "many people came to Detroit."

☐ c. "In the 1800s" reports *Detroit Now*, "many people came to Detroit."

**8** Which direct quotation uses correct punctuation?

☐ a. Dr. Anderson said, "Many immigrants come to the United States looking for work".

☐ b. "Dr. Anderson said, Many immigrants come to the United States looking for work."

☐ c. Dr. Anderson said, "Many immigrants come to the United States looking for work."

**9** Which direct quotation uses correct punctuation?

☐ a. "Many people from Latin America live in California," says historian Eva Arroyo, "as well as in Texas."

☐ b. "Many people from Latin America live in California, says historian Eva Arroyo, as well as in Texas".

☐ c. "Many people from Latin America live in California" says historian Eva Arroyo "as well as in Texas."

**10** Which direct quotation uses correct punctuation?

☐ a. "Could it be easier for younger people to adjust," asks Lisa, "or is it just as difficult at any age?"

☐ b. "Could it be easier for younger people to adjust," asks Lisa, or is it just as difficult at any age?

☐ c. "Could it be easier for younger people to adjust?" asks Lisa, "or is it just as difficult at any age"?

## Strategies to Avoid Repetition of Words

**Connecting to the Theme**

Group interviews are becoming more popular when interviewing candidates for a job. What could be the reasons for this? Which of these apply?

**A** Teamwork is becoming more important in the workplace.

**B** If more people are involved in the interview process, it is less likely that a "bad" candidate will be hired.

**C** It allows interviewers to see how potential employees interact with other people.

*All are valid reasons.*

## A. Skill Presentation

Repeating key ideas in a paragraph helps make the sentences flow together smoothly, but repeating the same key words will make your writing repetitive. There are a number of ways to avoid this.

One technique is to replace key words with synonyms or to use pronouns to refer to them. Look at this paragraph about group interviews. **Key words** are repeated too often.

> When conducting group interviews, the **interviewers** at Harrison Global Web Design have a clear **objective**. The **interviewers** give a group of candidates a **task**, but the **task** is not completely clear. In addition, there is a time limit. The **objective** is to see how well the candidates work together under pressure.

Now look at the revised paragraph with **synonyms** and pronouns replacing some of the key words.

> When conducting group interviews, the **interviewers** at Harrison Global Web Design have a clear **objective**. They give a group of candidates a **task**, but it is not completely clear. In addition, there is a time limit. The **goal** is to see how well the candidates work together under pressure.

Another technique is to use different word forms to say the same thing in a slightly different way. In this paragraph about group interviews, the writer uses the adjective form of *simulation – simulated –* to avoid repeating the noun.

> JV Corporation often uses a simulation to evaluate candidates' personalities. When a group of candidates watch and respond to a simulated conflict situation, for example, the interviewers can clearly see how creatively each individual thinks.

# B. Over to You

**1** **Read the sentences from a paragraph about preparing for a group interview, and answer the questions.**

To prepare for a group interview, do Internet research and talk to anyone you know who works for the company. During the interview, find opportunities to ask the interviewers questions that demonstrate your knowledge. If you show them what you know about the company, you will stand out from the crowd.

**1** Which synonym has the writer used for the word *demonstrate*? _____

**2** Which phrase has the writer used instead of the word *knowledge*? _____

**3** Which pronoun has the writer used to refer to *interviewers*? _____

**2** **Read the sentences and decide if they are repetitive or not. Write *R* for Repetitive or *NR* for Not Repetitive.**

___ **1** Do not expect small organizations to offer group interviews. Usually, only large companies can afford them.

___ **2** Researching the company before an interview is important. Talking to people who work for the company in addition to researching the company is also important.

___ **3** If possible, introduce yourself to the interviewers. You may stand out from the group more if you introduce yourself to the interviewers.

___ **4** It is a good idea to demonstrate leadership skills in a group. One way to show your leadership skills in a group is to be an active listener.

___ **5** Make sure you understand the duties of the job. If you are not aware of the job responsibilities, you may not succeed in the interview.

___ **6** Successful candidates make eye contact with the others in the group. Making eye contact with the interviewers is another characteristic of successful candidates.

___ **7** You might be asked to introduce yourself in a group interview. Therefore, it is advisable to prepare a short presentation about your background and experiences before the meeting.

___ **8** Afterward, make sure to thank the interviewers. In addition, be sure to show your appreciation of the other candidates.

___ **9** Pay close attention to any instructions. In order to impress the interviewers, you will have to show that you can follow complex directions.

___ **10** Remember to smile. Smiling indicates friendliness and confidence.

## CHECK!

To avoid too much repetition of words in your writing:

**1** replace key words with _____.

**2** use _____ to refer to key words.

**3** use different _____ _____ to say the same thing in a different way.

# C. Practice

**1** Match the sentences (1–5) with a sentence from the same paragraph (a–e). Look for synonyms, pronouns, and different word forms to help you.

___ **1** Small companies rarely use group interviews, which tend to be expensive.

___ **2** Sometimes another candidate in a group interview brings up a point that you had intended to make.

___ **3** First impressions are crucial in group interviews.

___ **4** Group interviews can seem stressful.

___ **5** Smile and appear confident when you participate in a group interview.

**a** Instead, they tend to favor individual interviews.

**b** Therefore, make a conscious effort to impress the interviewers as soon as you meet.

**c** An appearance that conveys friendliness and confidence is one of the keys to interviewing success.

**d** When another interviewee does this, be sure to comment on his or her idea.

**e** However, if you view them simply as an opportunity to interact with a group of people, you may experience less anxiety.

**2** Read the paragraph and decide if the writer uses synonyms, pronouns, and different word forms to avoid repeating key words. Write *YES* or *NO*.

Showing that you are a team player is important in a group interview. Good team players share a number of personal qualities. One important personal quality that team players have in common is being a good listener. Companies value people who can actively listen to the ideas of others. People who can actively listen are better able to understand and summarize ideas. They do this without judging or arguing with ideas that are different from their own. Essentially, good team players listen first and then speak. Carefully considering information before acting on it is an essential skill for teamwork.

_____

**Now complete the same paragraph with the correct words and phrases.**

**active listeners**     **characteristic**     **individuals who excel at teamwork**

**people who work well on a team**

Showing that you are a team player is important in a group interview. Good team players share a number of personal qualities. One important [1]_____ that [2]_____ have in common is being a good listener. Companies value people who can actively listen to the ideas of others. [3]_____ are better able to understand and summarize ideas. They do this without judging or arguing with ideas that are different from their own. Essentially, [4]_____ listen first and then speak. Carefully considering information before acting on it is an essential skill for teamwork in the workplace.

# D. Skill Quiz

**Check (✓) the correct answer for each item.**

1  In your writing, it is important to
- ☐ a. use the same words frequently to repeat key ideas.
- ☐ b. repeat key ideas without overusing the same words.
- ☐ c. avoid repeating key ideas and words.

2  What is one way to avoid repetition?
- ☐ a. give examples
- ☐ b. add new ideas
- ☐ c. use synonyms

3  Which part of speech can help avoid overusing nouns?
- ☐ a. pronouns
- ☐ b. prepositions
- ☐ c. articles

4  An example of using a different word form is
- ☐ a. using *she* for *the candidate*.
- ☐ b. using *show* instead of *showing*.
- ☐ c. using *business* for *company*.

5  *Some companies avoid phone interviews with job hunters. These businesses want to see candidates face-to-face.*
   *Businesses* is used to replace which word in the first sentence?
- ☐ a. interviews
- ☐ b. job hunters
- ☐ c. companies

6  *Employers notice candidates who are dressed well. Well-dressed job hunters tend to stand out to interviewers.*
   *Interviewers* is used to replace which word in the first sentence?
- ☐ a. employers
- ☐ b. candidates
- ☐ c. job hunters

7  *Successful candidates write thank-you letters to the interviewers. They do not simply send an e-mail.*
   *They* is used to replace which word or words in the first sentence?
- ☐ a. successful candidates
- ☐ b. thank-you letters
- ☐ c. interviewers

8  *Success depends on the ability to communicate well. In order to be successful, you must speak and write clearly.*
   The second sentence uses a different word form than the first sentence. This word is
- ☐ a. *clearly* for *well*
- ☐ b. *successful* for *success*
- ☐ c. *speak and write* for *communicate*

9  Which sentences best avoid repetition?
- ☐ a. Experts suggest learning about a company before an interview. For example, experts recommend reading the company's annual report.
- ☐ b. Experts suggest learning about a company before an interview. For example, they recommend studying its annual report.

10  Which sentences best avoids repetition?
- ☐ a. Employers are looking for people who are good problem solvers. Having problem-solving skills is an advantage in the job market.
- ☐ b. Employers are looking for people who are good problem solvers. People who are good problem solvers look attractive to most employers in the job market.

**CONNECTING TO THE THEME**

The Myers-Briggs Type Indicator (MBTI) is a personality test designed to understand how people see the world and make decisions. How can companies use this assessment tool?

**A** to hire the right people for the job
**B** to put together the best combination of team members
**C** to manage employees more effectively
**D** to help extroverts

*All are valid ways.*

## A. Skill Presentation

Academic writing should be concise – expressing only what needs to be said without using unnecessary words. Therefore, it is important to avoid **wordiness** and **redundancy**. Wordiness is the inclusion of unnecessary words. Redundancy is saying the same thing more than once. Unnecessary and redundant words should be removed.

Look at this example:

> Mr. Tanaka **searched for and** found some **extremely** interesting information about personality tests on the **online** website.  ✗

In this sentence, the phrase *searched for* is unnecessary. It is only important to know that Mr. Tanaka *found* this information. The word *extremely* is an intensifier – it doesn't add important information. The word *online* is redundant – all websites are online. Look at the revised sentence where these words have been deleted. It is now much more concise and has a clear, academic tone.

> Mr. Tanaka found some interesting information about personality tests on the website.  ✓

To avoid wordiness and redundancy in groups of sentences, sentences can sometimes be combined and revised to remove unnecessary information.

BUSINESS PERSONALITIES

Avoiding Wordiness and Redundancy

12

# B. Over to You

**1** **Read the sentence and check (✓) the technique that would remove the redundancy from the sentence.**

In general, extroverted people feel most satisfied when working with other people, and they get less satisfaction from working alone.

☐    a. Delete the pronoun *they*.
☐    b. Delete *and they get less satisfaction from working alone.*
☐    c. Change *when working with other people* to *when they work with other people.*

**2** **Read the sentence and check (✓) the technique that would make the sentence less wordy.**

Personality tests are not always completely accurate. However, even though this may be true, they can be a useful guide for someone choosing a career.

☐    a. Delete *However, even though this may be true*. Then combine the sentences with *but*.
☐    b. Change *However, even though this may be true* to *Although this may indeed be the case*.
☐    c. Delete the phrase *for someone choosing a career*.

**3** **Read the sentences and decide if they are wordy or contain redundancy. Write *YES* or *NO*.**

_____ **1** Personality tests can help people make decisions about which careers will most likely be compatible with their interests and abilities.

_____ **2** Some people like to think systematically about a problem, weighing the advantages and disadvantages and considering all the positive and negative outcomes in order to make a decision.

_____ **3** For certain people, considering their emotional reaction to an issue is an integral part of the decision-making process.

_____ **4** Some situations are ones that require and demand people to use logic rather than use feelings.

_____ **5** People who are identified as having strong "feeling" personality types are concerned about what is important to other people, and they show concern for others.

_____ **6** Individuals who are more concerned with others' feelings rather than the facts sometimes are not able to see the facts of a situation clearly because their emotions dominate.

## CHECK!

Avoid wordiness and redundancy in academic writing.

**1** _____ is the use of unnecessary words.

**2** _____ means saying the same thing more than once.

# C. Practice

**1** These sentences are wordy and contain redundancy. Read each sentence and a suggestion of how to improve it. Check (✓) if the suggestion will solve the problem.

  **1** Extroverts typically have many friends and enjoy expanding their social circle and getting to know new people.

    ☐   **Suggestion:** Delete *have many friends and*.

  **2** When they have a problem to solve at work, extroverts are likely to discuss it with colleagues and get co-workers' opinions.

    ☐   **Suggestion:** Delete *and get co-workers opinions*.

  **3** Sometimes extroverts jump into projects without considering what they hope to accomplish or developing a plan for what they hope to achieve.

    ☐   **Suggestion:** Delete *developing a plan for*.

  **4** Introverts very much prefer to rely on their own ideas rather than on other people's.

    ☐   **Suggestion:** Delete *very much*.

  **5** Introverts may spend a great deal of time thinking about how to solve a problem; as a result, their ideas about how to solve a problem sometimes take longer to put into action.

    ☐   **Suggestion:** Delete second *about how to solve a problem*.

**2** Read the sentences and check (✓) the best way to make them more concise.

  **1** In one part of the MBTI, an individual's personality is matched with one of two preferences – the two preferences are "sensing" and "intuition."

    ☐   a. Delete the phrase *of the MBTI*.
    ☐   b. Delete the phrase *the two preferences are*.

  **2** The majority of "sensing" individuals prefer a practical approach to tasks. They really feel it is important to understand the purpose of a new project before beginning.

    ☐   a. Delete the word *really*.
    ☐   b. Delete the clause *before beginning*.

  **3** People who are considered "sensing" types excel at remembering significant details.

    ☐   a. Delete the phrase *People who are considered*.
    ☐   b. Change the phrase *excel at* to *demonstrate proficiency when it comes to*.

  **4** Unlike "sensing" types, "intuitive" types actually feel that learning by experience is not ideal. It is interesting to note that they prefer to think through problems instead.

    ☐   a. Change the phrase *is not ideal* to *is less than ideal*.
    ☐   b. Delete the words *actually* and *It is interesting to note that*.

  **5** "Sensing" people gather facts and then form a big picture. The opposite is true of "intuitive" types. "Intuitive" types are different because they prefer to first understand the big picture and then learn the details.

    ☐   a. Delete the sentence *"Sensing" people gather facts and then form a big picture*.
    ☐   b. Delete the sentence *"Intuitive" types are different because they prefer to first understand the big picture and then learn the details*.

# D. Skill Quiz

**Check (✓) the correct answer for each item.**

**1** Academic writing should
- ☐ a. contain long sentences.
- ☐ b. be concise.
- ☐ c. use a lot of intensifiers.

**2** A wordy sentence
- ☐ a. is frequently too short.
- ☐ b. includes more than one main idea.
- ☐ c. includes unnecessary words.

**3** Redundancy is
- ☐ a. combining two simple sentences.
- ☐ b. expressing the same idea two or more times.
- ☐ c. explaining an idea clearly and completely.

**4** One way to avoid wordiness is to avoid using
- ☐ a. pronouns and adjectives.
- ☐ b. time clauses.
- ☐ c. intensifiers like *really* and *very*.

**5** Another way to avoid wordiness is to
- ☐ a. combine sentences when possible.
- ☐ b. use only action verbs.
- ☐ c. explain things clearly by repeating important information.

**6** Choose the most concise option.
- ☐ a. The MBTI is based on the theories of a psychiatrist named Jung. Jung developed theories that contribute to this test.
- ☐ b. The MBTI is partially based on the theories of psychological types that were described and explained by a psychiatrist named Jung.
- ☐ c. The MBTI draws on the theories of psychological types developed by psychiatrist Jung.

**7** Choose the most concise option.
- ☐ a. Introverts rarely choose to work in groups but often prove to be productive team members.
- ☐ b. It is rare that introverts choose to work in groups, but they are often productive team members.
- ☐ c. Introverts may prove to be productive team members, and they may make positive contributions to groups at work.

**8** Choose the most concise option.
- ☐ a. People should have careers compatible with their own ways of thinking and with their own ways of making decisions.
- ☐ b. People should have careers compatible with their own ways of thinking and making decisions.
- ☐ c. People should have careers that they feel to be compatible with their own specific work styles.

**9** Choose the most concise option.
- ☐ a. Carl Jung is widely considered to be a founder of psychology. He was born in 1875 and died in 1961.
- ☐ b. Carl Jung, considered a founder of psychology, was born in 1875 and died in 1961.
- ☐ c. Carl Jung, who was a founder of psychology, was born in 1875 and then he died in 1961.

**10** Choose the most concise option.
- ☐ a. Jung's theory was that people's behavior is consistent. It is not random.
- ☐ b. Jung's theory was that people's behavior is consistent, not random.
- ☐ c. Jung's theory was that people's behavior is consistently the same. Their behavior is not random.

GENETICALLY MODIFIED FOOD

### CONNECTING TO THE THEME

How much do you know about genetically modified (GM) food? The DNA of some plants and animals can be changed to produce food that has certain advantages. Are these statements about GM food true or false?

**1** Food can be genetically modified so that it is not affected by bad weather or insects.

**2** The amount of GM food the world is eating is decreasing.

**3** The long-term effects of GM food have not been thoroughly researched yet.

**4** Food can be genetically modified to include more vitamins or other nutrients.

*Answers: 1 True, 2 False, 3 True, 4 True.*

## A. Skill Presentation

Spelling words correctly is crucial in academic writing. Be aware of words that are frequently misspelled in English. Study the charts below.

| WORDS WITH DOUBLE CONSONANTS | | WORDS THAT SOUND DIFFERENT FROM THEIR SPELLING | |
|---|---|---|---|
| ✗ | ✓ | ✗ | ✓ |
| acording | according | calender | calendar |
| atractive | attractive | fisical | physical |
| inteligent | intelligent | grammer | grammar |
| oportunity | opportunity | maybee | maybe |
| recomend | recommend | negoshiate | negotiate |

| WORDS WITH SILENT LETTERS | | WORDS WITH THE COMBINATION *i-e* OR *e-i* | |
|---|---|---|---|
| ✗ | ✓ | ✗ | ✓ |
| tecnique | technique | acheive | achieve |
| wether | whether | beleive | believe |
| busness | business | freind | friend |
| enviroment | environment | cieling | ceiling |
| nowlege | knowledge | recieve | receive |

Words that have similar *spellings* but different *pronunciations* and *meanings* are frequently confused. Be sure you choose the word with the correct meaning. Look at these examples.

advice – advise    woman – women    desert – dessert    lose – loose

Words that sound alike but are spelled differently and have different meanings are frequently confused. Be sure you choose the word with the correct spelling for the meaning you want. Look at these examples.

affect – effect    capital – capitol    cite – sight – site    hear – here
its – it's    passed – past    principal – principle    their – there – they're

# B. Over to You

**1   Read the paragraph about organic food, and circle the correctly spelled words.**

Many people ¹*beleive* | *believe* eating organic food ²*affects* | *effects* your health. They think it is ³*necessary* | *necesary* to eat organic food to be healthy. Growing organic food can also be good for the ⁴*enviroment* | *environment*. Other people think that eating organic food is ⁵*similar* | *similer* to eating non-organic food, and there are no real ⁶*benefits* | *benifits*.

**2   Read the sentences. The words in bold are all misspelled. Write the correct words.**

1   The agricultural organization offers **advise** on how to avoid genetically modified foods for people who choose not to eat them. _____

2   Food labels are not likely to indicate that a product is genetically modified, but a product that is not genetically modified may indicate this on **it's** label. _____

3   Natural or organic food stores offer a variety of fresh produce. These types of stores **usualy** do not carry GM foods. _____

4   Purchasing produce at a farmer's market is appealing to some consumers because they can speak with farmers directly to find out if **there** food is genetically modified. _____

5   A conversation with a local farmer may reveal **wether** or not man-made pesticides were used to grow the crops. _____

6   Several local neighborhood organizations maintain food-related websites. In addition to general information about local farms, they post **calenders** with dates for local markets.

_____

7   It can be challenging to make decisions about which kinds of foods are best for you, since they involve personal decisions. Getting information and advice from **freinds** can make these choices easier. _____

8   Genetically modified foods are a fairly recent addition to the North American market, having been introduced in the early 1990s. In the **passed**, consumers did not have as many choices. _____

---

## CHECK!

It is important to spell words correctly. Watch out for:

**1**   words with double _____.

**2**   words that sound different from their _____.

**3**   words with _____ letters.

**4**   words with the combination _____ or _____.

# C. Practice

**1** **Read the sentences and decide which of the words in each sentence is misspelled. Write _A_, _B_, or _C_.**

___ **1** [A]Allthough not everyone agrees, one [B]technique that may contribute to good [C]overall health is to include organic fruits and vegetables in your diet.

___ **2** Because organic food is [A]percieved as having certain health [B]benefits, it is an [C]attractive option for many people.

___ **3** One expert claims, "It is [A]increaseingly easy to find organic foods." She goes on to say that [B]maybe this is because people are demanding these products in their [C]supermarkets.

___ **4** In the 1990s, the amount of organic eggs and milk [A]began to increase in [B]addition to the amount of organic fruits and [C]vegtables.

___ **5** [A]According to a reporter, one local organic supermarket is in need of urgent repairs. The building is old, and the [B]ceiling is [C]leeking.

___ **6** The reporter exposed problems with the local supermarket after [A]severel [B]neighbors joined together to draw attention to the [C]issues.

___ **7** The organic supermarket is a local [A]busines that most residents support. They [B]appreciate having a [C]convenient source of fresh produce.

___ **8** Organic food stores are [A]common in [B]sertain [C]regions, such as urban areas.

**2** **Read each sentence in the chart. If it is correct, check (✓) the box. If it includes a misspelled word, write the word correctly in the box.**

| | |
|---|---|
| 1. It is generally a good idea to have nowledge about organic food even if you choose not to eat it. | |
| 2. Some say that organic food has a number of positive physical effects, including improved health and increased longevity. | |
| 3. Experts recomend that people who wish to avoid man-made pesticides entirely should buy only organic vegetables. | |
| 4. Some health professionals suggest buying organic meat and dairy products if you beleive giving hormones to animals is undesirable. | |
| 5. Many people buy organic food because they do not agree with the principle of using pesticides. | |
| 6. Foods that have been treated with chemicals loose their flavor. | |
| 7. Organically grown food can be good for the environment because it tends to create less polution than other methods. | |
| 8. Some people do not have the opportunity to buy organic food in the areas where they live. | |
| 9. When consumors purchase produce from local farmers, the money usually goes directly to the farm. | |

# D. Skill Quiz

**Check (✓) the correct answer for each item.**

1 Words like *hear* and *here* are easily confused because
- [ ] a. they have more than one vowel.
- [ ] b. they sound the same but are spelled differently.
- [ ] c. they have silent letters.

2 Words like *millennium* and *recommend* are often misspelled because
- [ ] a. they have double consonants.
- [ ] b. they are not common words in English.
- [ ] c. they have silent letters.

3 Choose the correct word to complete this sentence: *More people are buying organic foods than in the ___.*
- [ ] a. passed
- [ ] b. past
- [ ] c. pass

4 Choose the correct word to complete this sentence: *___ store only sells organic products.*
- [ ] a. There
- [ ] b. They're
- [ ] c. Their

5 Choose the correct word to complete this sentence: *FoodMap.gov is a ___ on the Internet where you can find out about healthy food choices.*
- [ ] a. site
- [ ] b. cite
- [ ] c. sight

6 Choose the correct word to complete this sentence: *My sister only bakes ___ with organic ingredients.*
- [ ] a. disserts
- [ ] b. deserts
- [ ] c. desserts

7 Choose the correct word to complete this sentence: *The large plant that produces GM foods is located in the state ___.*
- [ ] a. capitol.
- [ ] b. capatal.
- [ ] c. capital.

8 Choose the correct word to complete this sentence: *Can you ___ prices at a farmer's market?*
- [ ] a. negotiate
- [ ] b. negoshiate
- [ ] c. negosiate

9 Choose the correct word to complete this sentence: *It is possible to ___ e-mails about new genetically modified foods on the market.*
- [ ] a. recieve
- [ ] b. receive
- [ ] c. reiceve

10 Choose the correct word to complete this sentence: *___ to Dr. Perry, genetically modified food can help fight starvation.*
- [ ] a. According
- [ ] b. Acording
- [ ] c. Acordding

## CHILDREN AND HEALTH

## A. Skill Presentation

A **fact** is something that is true and can be proven. An **opinion** is someone's feelings or beliefs about something. Look at these sentences.

**FACT:** Research shows that home-cooked meals usually include more fruits and vegetables than meals in restaurants.

**OPINION:** Home-cooked meals taste better than meals in restaurants.

Facts help make writing more objective and impersonal. You should include them in academic writing. Remember that many facts require a citation to provide details about where the information came from.

If you do include opinions in your writing, for example, when you make an argument in an essay, use facts to support the opinions and make them stronger and more objective.

Look at this excerpt from an academic essay about parents eating meals with their children. It expresses the writer's **opinion** that parents should eat with their children. The writer then uses **facts** to support the idea. This makes the writing stronger and more objective.

[O]Parents should eat at least one meal a day with their children. [F]Research shows that there are many benefits when a family eats together. [F]Several studies by Becky Hand, a dietician, have indicated that children are healthier when they eat five to six meals a week with their parents.

# B. Over to You

**1** **Read the sentences and decide which one expresses a fact and which one expresses an opinion. Write *FACT* or *OPINION*.**

1 _____: Teenagers who do not do well in school are lazy.

2 _____: One study showed that teenagers who ate meals with their families did well academically.

**2** **Read each statement in the chart, and decide if it is a fact or an opinion. Check (✓) the box in the correct column.**

| | FACT | OPINION |
|---|---|---|
| 1. Green vegetables taste better than other vegetables. | | |
| 2. The U.S. Department of Agriculture recommends that adults eat two to three cups of vegetables per day. | | |
| 3. People who are overweight should make an effort to reduce the number of calories they consume. | | |
| 4. Research indicates that a diet low in salt can help people lower their blood pressure. | | |
| 5. *Beyond Fat* is a reality-based television show about teens who are taking steps toward losing weight. | | |
| 6. *Less than Skinny* was the most entertaining show on television. | | |
| 7. People who participate in weight-loss competitions are not serious about changing their health habits. | | |
| 8. Some companies hold competitions to help their employees lose weight. | | |
| 9. The U.S. Department of Agriculture emphasizes that exercise is an important part of being healthy and reducing stress. | | |
| 10. Playing a team sport is a better way to exercise than working out in a gym. | | |

## CHECK!

**1** Academic writing should include _____ to make it more objective.
A _____ is something that is true and can be proven.

**2** An _____ is someone's feelings or beliefs about a topic. If you do include _____, make sure they are supported by facts.

# C. Practice

**1** **Match each opinion (1–6) with the sentence that contains a fact to support it (a–f).**

___ **1** Adults should help children learn about healthy eating habits.

___ **2** Americans should take better care of their hearts.

___ **3** Consumers who read nutrition fact labels on food products are better able to make informed decisions about nutrition.

___ **4** Strenuous exercise is not beneficial for everyone.

___ **5** Fried food is extremely unhealthy and can lead to heart problems.

___ **6** By not exercising enough, people may gain too much weight.

**a** About 80 million adults in the United States currently suffer from heart disease, according to the American Heart Association.

**b** For example, the U.S. Department of Agriculture (USDA) recommends that people who are at risk for heart disease consult a doctor before exercising.

**c** The Food and Drug Administration (FDA) strongly supports the claim that parents and teachers can fight unhealthy weight gain by teaching children about eating better.

**d** The Food and Drug Administration says that healthier choices include lean meats that are baked, boiled, or grilled.

**e** The USDA advises most people to exercise for 60 minutes a day to prevent weight gain that may lead to serious health problems.

**f** Shirley Blakely, a dietician, stresses that shoppers who understand what is in their food can more clearly see the connections between ingredients and health.

**2** **Read the paragraph about cooking and children. Decide if statements 1–6 are the writer's opinion or if they are supported by fact. Write *O* for Opinion or *F* for Fact.**

### Cooking Together

Learning how to cook is an important skill that all children should learn. According to dietician Becky Hand, many children today do not know how to plan and prepare meals. Research shows that learning how to cook leads to increased independence. Parents should therefore teach their children how to cook. Hand suggests that young children can help with simple tasks, such as cutting soft foods, and older children can assist with more difficult tasks like grilling food. One easy recipe is grilled chicken, which is easy to prepare and tastes delicious. Even if the recipes are simple, research shows that children who cook with their parents learn valuable skills.

___ **1** All children should learn to cook.

___ **2** Children do not know how to prepare meals.

___ **3** Children who can cook become more independent.

___ **4** It is important for parents to teach children how to cook.

___ **5** Grilled chicken tastes delicious.

___ **6** Children learn valuable skills by cooking with their parents.

# D. Skill Quiz

**Check (✓) the correct answer for each item.**

1 A fact is something
  ☐ a. that one person believes.
  ☐ b. that can be proven.
  ☐ c. that most people agree about.

2 What is an opinion?
  ☐ a. one person's belief about a topic
  ☐ b. common knowledge or a general truth
  ☐ c. something that can be proven with data

3 What is one reason to include facts in an essay?
  ☐ a. Facts make your writing personal.
  ☐ b. Facts make your sentences longer.
  ☐ c. Facts help support the opinions you include.

4 Which word is often associated with facts used to support opinions?
  ☐ a. belief
  ☐ b. research
  ☐ c. style

5 Choose the sentence that expresses an opinion.
  ☐ a. A few tablespoons of chocolate syrup improves the taste of milk significantly.
  ☐ b. Teenagers need more milk than children, according to many studies.
  ☐ c. Milk and cheese are products that are available in most grocery stores.

6 Choose the sentence that gives a fact.
  ☐ a. The USDA is an agency that advises Americans about food.
  ☐ b. The best job for a dietician is working for the USDA.
  ☐ c. The USDA's website is nicely designed and easy to use.

7 Choose the sentence that gives a fact.
  ☐ a. Fruit is the best choice for dessert after a heavy meal.
  ☐ b. According to a USDA study, adults should eat about two cups of fruit a day.
  ☐ c. All children love fruit.

8 *Exercising for 60 minutes every day is an easy goal to achieve.*
  Which fact best supports this opinion?
  ☐ a. Walking to work every morning is the easiest way to get exercise.
  ☐ b. Sixty minutes of exercise can be done 20 minutes at a time, making it easier to fit into busy schedules.
  ☐ c. The USDA says people need to combine smart food choices with exercise in order to be healthy.

9 *Parents should make an effort to eat dinner with their children.*
  Which fact best supports this opinion?
  ☐ a. One study revealed that healthy meals include a lot of vegetables.
  ☐ b. Children who eat dinner with their parents seem to appreciate it.
  ☐ c. There are many benefits for children who eat with their families, according to new research.

10 *It is important for adults to prioritize the maintenance of low cholesterol levels.*
  Which fact best supports this opinion?
  ☐ a. Some people have noticed a recent trend toward low-fat diets.
  ☐ b. Studies show that elevated cholesterol levels are closely linked with heart disease.
  ☐ c. Cholesterol tests are inexpensive enough so that everyone can afford one.

## CONNECTING TO THE THEME

Looking for medical advice on the Internet can be a fast, inexpensive method of getting a diagnosis. However, it may lead to an incorrect diagnosis or the wrong treatment. What is your opinion of using the Internet to self-diagnose?

**A** It can be useful, but it should always be followed by a visit to the doctor.

**B** Going to the doctor is a waste of time when symptoms can be researched in this way.

**C** There is no substitute for visiting a doctor.

**D** It may encourage hypochondria or severe health anxiety.

## A. Skill Presentation

When you make an argument in your writing, you can include **opinions** as long as they are supported with facts and examples. It is important to acknowledge opposing opinions – opinions that are different from your own – because it shows that you have researched the topic thoroughly and considered other points of view. It is also important to include a refutation – a response to the opposing opinion. It brings readers back to and strengthens your original opinion.

Look at these sentences from an essay on physical and psychological illnesses. The writer has expressed her opinion first and then expressed the opposing opinion. The writer finishes by including a refutation that refers back to the opposing opinion. The refutation acknowledges that hypochondria does occasionally take up a doctor's time, but it strengthens the opinion by arguing that hypochondria is a real disease.

[O]Doctors must give the same attention to psychological illnesses, such as hypochondria, as they do to physical illnesses. [OO]However, some may argue that treating hypochondriacs wastes valuable consultation time that could otherwise be spent on patients with serious physical problems. [R]While hypochondria may take up a physician's time, it is important to keep in mind that psychological illnesses like hypochondria can, in fact, develop into physical conditions.

# B. Over to You

**1  Read the paragraph about self-diagnosis over the Internet, and answer the questions.**

[A]Increasingly, people are turning to the Internet to research symptoms when they feel ill. [B]It is dangerous for people to self-diagnose over the Internet because there is a lot of medical misinformation on the Internet. [C]On the other hand, a person who researches symptoms online before going to the doctor may get more out of his or her visit. [D]Even though these patients may be more informed, using the Internet to self-diagnose tends to cause hypochondria and may lead to unnecessary anxiety.

| | | | | |
|---|---|---|---|---|
| **1** Which sentence expresses the writer's opinion? | **A** | **B** | **C** | **D** |
| **2** Which sentence is the opposing opinion? | **A** | **B** | **C** | **D** |
| **3** Which sentence is the refutation? | **A** | **B** | **C** | **D** |

**2  Match the writer's opinions (1–6) with the correct opposing opinions (a–f).**

____ **1** In the United States, most doctors' salaries are higher than necessary.

____ **2** Search engines should be built to guide users to accurate medical information on the Internet.

____ **3** Everyone in the United States should have health insurance.

____ **4** Adults who are experiencing any symptoms that make them physically uncomfortable should visit their doctor immediately.

____ **5** In general, medical students who suffer from anxiety may not become confident doctors.

____ **6** Medical schools should include a course on treating patients who suffer from hypochondria.

**a** On the other hand, it can be argued that people have the right to search for any information regarding their health, whether it is correct or not.

**b** However, to avoid wasting consultation time, it may be beneficial for these people to call first and describe their symptoms over the phone.

**c** Medical school, however, is expensive, and many doctors must pay back large loans.

**d** On the other hand, there are many more important ailments that medical students should be studying.

**e** However, it is virtually impossible to force people to purchase insurance if they do not believe it is necessary.

**f** It is important to note, however, that medical students' stress levels often drop significantly as soon as they graduate and begin their new careers.

## CHECK!

**1** When you make an argument in your writing, state your opinion and follow it with an _____ _____ that is different from your own.

**2** Add a _____ to respond and make your opinion stronger.

# C. Practice

**1 Read each opinion and decide if the second sentence is an opposing argument or a refutation. Write *OA* for Opposing Argument or *R* for Refutation.**

1 A person who suffers from anxiety should not attend medical school.

___ However, it could be considered unethical to discriminate against people with emotional illnesses.

2 Medical students should be required to learn a foreign language.

___ Although medical students already have full schedules, knowing a second language would improve their communication with patients.

3 It is dangerous to treat anxiety with drugs alone.

___ In spite of this, medications have been proven to help many mentally ill people.

4 Cross-cultural training courses are a waste of medical students' time.

___ On the other hand, doctors treat patients from a variety of cultural backgrounds and must be sensitive to different approaches to treatment.

5 Drug companies should be forbidden to advertise their products on television.

___ Even though some of these medications may be effective, the commercials may lead to people becoming overmedicated.

6 Health insurance should pay for cosmetic surgery.

___ Although many cosmetic procedures are unnecessary, they are often important for emotional well-being.

7 Laws should prevent the use of animals in drug experiments.

___ While it is dangerous to use human subjects, there are other ways to test new drugs without harming animals.

8 Ignoring symptoms can be very dangerous.

___ On the other hand, it is a mistake to take all symptoms too seriously.

**2 Number the sentences in the correct order. Put the opinion first, the opposing opinion second, and the refutation third.**

1 ___ However, restricting Internet access in the United States violates individuals' rights.

___ That being said, medical websites should monitor their content so people can distinguish accurate information from inaccurate information.

___ It is crucial that access to medical information on the Internet be more heavily restricted.

2 ___ Even though people believe they are really ill, it is important to remember that medical websites may contain incorrect information.

___ People who have consulted the Internet to self-diagnose a serious illness should think twice before wasting a doctor's consultation time.

___ On the other hand, well-informed patients may be able to accurately diagnose symptoms of a serious illness themselves.

# D. Skill Quiz

**Check (✓) the correct answer for each item.**

1 An opinion that is different from yours is
- ☐ a. an opposing opinion.
- ☐ b. a refutation.
- ☐ c. a fact.

2 Adding an opposing opinion
- ☐ a. strengthens your argument.
- ☐ b. weakens your argument.
- ☐ c. makes your argument too complicated.

3 A refutation
- ☐ a. explains all the reasons why the opposing opinion is incorrect.
- ☐ b. acknowledges the opposing opinion but restates and strengthens your opinion.
- ☐ c. shows that you understand why your opinion is weak.

4 A word such as *however* often
- ☐ a. introduces any facts you give.
- ☐ b. introduces your opinion.
- ☐ c. introduces an opposing opinion.

5 Which sentence states the writer's opinion?
- ☐ a. However, misinformation can cause confusion and anxiety.
- ☐ b. Some information is incorrect, but studies show people who stay informed have fewer diseases.
- ☐ c. The best way to avoid illness is to be informed about a variety of health topics.

6 Choose the refutation.
- ☐ a. However, many doctors simply do not have the time to give much attention to their patients.
- ☐ b. Even though doctors are overworked, patients deserve a doctor's full attention.
- ☐ c. Doctors should increase the time they spend with patients.

7 Choose the opposing opinion.
- ☐ a. Some people, on the other hand, are good at making self-diagnoses.
- ☐ b. Treating oneself for an illness based on an online article can be extremely dangerous.
- ☐ c. It is a mistake for individuals to diagnose their own illness.

8 Choose the opposing opinion to: *Hypochondriacs waste doctors' time.*
- ☐ a. However, many hypochondriacs have imaginary ailments.
- ☐ b. However, many hypochondriacs do have real ailments.
- ☐ c. However, many hypochondriacs are wasting their doctor's time.

9 Choose the opposing opinion to: *One way to reduce the cost of healthcare is to teach children good lifestyle habits.*
- ☐ a. However, exercise and good nutrition lead to better health.
- ☐ b. That being said, having good lifestyle habits from an early age leads to better lifelong health.
- ☐ c. On the other hand, some people often do not have access to nutritious food and recreation.

10 Choose the refutation to: *In spite of this, medical websites are dangerous because they create anxiety.*
- ☐ a. Although some people can identify inaccurate information, it is true that hypochondria has increased since the start of the Internet.
- ☐ b. Even though using the Internet to self-diagnose can cause problems, most people are intelligent enough to evaluate what they read.
- ☐ c. In any case, the Internet is not a good source of medical information.

# 16

## Avoiding Choppy Sentences and Stringy Sentences

### CONNECTING TO THE THEME

**How healthy is your lifestyle?**

Leading a healthy lifestyle is important. This is especially true when students are away at college. It is well known that students often develop unhealthy habits that last beyond school and prove hard to break. Here are a few tips students can follow. How many are true for you?

- eat a balanced diet
- exercise regularly
- have a group of supportive friends
- get plenty of rest
- avoid too much stress

*0–1: you need to improve. 2–3: you're doing okay. 4–5: you're doing well!*

## A. Skill Presentation

In academic writing, it is important to avoid choppy sentences and stringy sentences.

**Choppy** sentences are short, simple sentences. In certain situations they can be effective, for example, when you want to grab your reader's attention and make a strong statement. However, a paragraph with too many choppy sentences can often be difficult to read. The sentences do not flow together well because nothing makes one sentence relate to the next. To improve choppy sentences, you can use **connectors**, such as *and, but, so, because,* and *however* to make compound or complex sentences. Look at this paragraph and how the writer improved it.

> Exercise is important. People should exercise every day. Walking is an effective form of exercise. Swimming is effective, too. ✗
>
> **Because** exercise is important, people should exercise every day. Walking **and** swimming are effective forms of exercise. ✓

**Stringy** sentences have too many clauses joined by connectors. They are often difficult to read because readers have to hold so much information in their minds at one time. To improve stringy sentences, divide them into shorter sentences, and use appropriate transition words and phrases. Look at this paragraph and how the writer improved it.

> A healthy lifestyle is important because it can help increase life expectancy, and having a balanced diet can prevent certain diseases while providing a sense of well-being, and healthy people tend to have more fulfilling lives. ✗
>
> A healthy lifestyle is important because it can help increase life expectancy. Having a balanced diet can also prevent certain diseases while providing a sense of well-being. **In addition**, healthy people tend to have more fulfilling lives. ✓

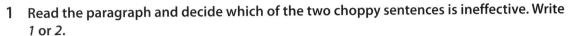

# B. Over to You

**1** **Read the paragraph and decide which of the two choppy sentences is ineffective. Write *1* or *2*.**

¹Clean drinking water is important. In cities, drinking water is often purified and distributed to the inhabitants. Residents therefore have convenient access to a safe source of water. ²Clean water prevents disease. ___

**2** **Read each sentence in the chart, and decide if it is choppy, stringy, or not choppy or stringy. Check (✓) the box in the correct column.**

| | CHOPPY | STRINGY | NOT CHOPPY OR STRINGY |
|---|---|---|---|
| 1. People should exercise more. | | | |
| 2. Fast food contains few nutrients, and it is often high in fat, so people should reduce their fast food consumption. | | | |
| 3. Vegetables are rich in nutrients, so they are beneficial, and adults should eat them regularly. | | | |
| 4. Children need calcium. | | | |
| 5. Avoiding caffeine and excess sugar, combined with activities, such as yoga, can help eliminate anxiety. | | | |
| 6. Doctors recommend that people consume enough vitamin D and that they be especially careful in the winter because the sun creates vitamin D, and people tend to get less sun in the winter. | | | |
| 7. Doctors are usually right. | | | |
| 8. Stress affects health. | | | |
| 9. Check-ups can reveal problems, so most adults should make regular appointments even if they are not sick, and doctors should examine them thoroughly. | | | |
| 10. Since clean water prevents diseases, countries should invest in water purification systems. | | | |

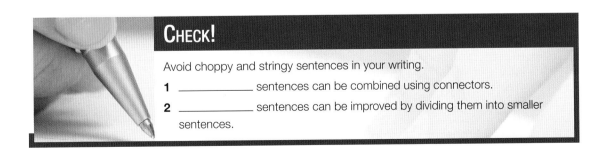

## CHECK!

Avoid choppy and stringy sentences in your writing.

**1** _____ sentences can be combined using connectors.

**2** _____ sentences can be improved by dividing them into smaller sentences.

# C. Practice

**1** Check (✓) the best correction for these choppy sentences.

1 Making healthy choices is important. So is living a healthy lifestyle. These things increase life expectancy.

☐ a. By choosing to live a healthy lifestyle, people can expect to live longer. This is one reason why making healthy choices is important.

☐ b. Life expectancy is higher among those who live a healthy lifestyle because their choices make them healthier overall, so they tend to get fewer illnesses.

☐ c. A healthy lifestyle incorporates exercise, and it also incorporates eating healthfully, because doing just one of these things does not necessarily increase life expectancy.

2 Smoking cigarettes is unhealthy. Smokers are advised to quit. Smoking can cause serious diseases. One such disease is lung cancer.

☐ a. Smoking can lead to lung cancer, which is one reason why it is considered unhealthy, so smokers are advised to quit.

☐ b. Because smoking can lead to serious diseases like lung cancer, most people consider cigarettes to be unhealthy. For this reason, smokers are advised to quit.

☐ c. Doctors recommend that smokers stop smoking cigarettes in order to avoid serious consequences, such as a heart attack or a stroke. Doctors generally agree that cigarettes are unhealthy.

**2** Read the stringy sentences and the suggestions to correct them. Decide if the sentences are improved and write *YES* or *NO*.

1 Ronda and her husband started a diet together, and they lost weight, so they felt healthier, which helped keep both of them motivated.

_____ **Suggestion**: Ronda and her husband started a diet. They wanted to lose weight. They wanted to get healthy. They supported each other. Ronda and her husband stayed motivated.

2 Some people take walks every day because they do not have time to go to the gym, but they want to exercise, so they take walks instead.

_____ **Suggestion**: Many people do not have time to go to the gym every day. Instead, they take walks as a way to get the exercise they need.

3 Relaxation reduces stress, which is one reason it is important for most people, and incorporating relaxing activities like reading or resting into your life can be simple.

_____ **Suggestion**: Relaxation is important because it reduces stress for most people. People who adjust their lifestyles to incorporate reading and resting are generally happier than those who do not.

4 Germs spread easily from one person to another, but some germs can be avoided, so to be safe, it is generally recommended that people wash their hands regularly and cover their mouths when they cough.

_____ **Suggestion**: Germs are easy to spread. It's possible to avoid certain germs. Washing your hands regularly can help. Covering your mouth when you cough also helps.

# D. Skill Quiz

**Check (✓) the correct answer for each item.**

1 Choppy sentences
- [ ] a. tend to make writing flow better.
- [ ] b. have too many connectors.
- [ ] c. are short, simple sentences.

2 What is one way to fix choppy sentences?
- [ ] a. Combine them using connectors like *and*, *but*, or *because*.
- [ ] b. Turn them into stringy sentences.
- [ ] c. Divide them into shorter sentences.

3 A choppy sentence can be useful when
- [ ] a. it is not possible to use *and* or *but*.
- [ ] b. you wish to grab your reader's attention.
- [ ] c. you do not wish to make a strong statement.

4 A choppy sentence can also be useful when
- [ ] a. making a strong statement.
- [ ] b. it is not possible to use transition words or phrases.
- [ ] c. it is not possible to use *because*.

5 Stringy sentences
- [ ] a. have too many connectors.
- [ ] b. are short, simple sentences.
- [ ] c. are effective in academic writing.

6 What is one way to fix a stringy sentence?
- [ ] a. Add more connectors.
- [ ] b. Change the position of the clauses.
- [ ] c. Divide it into shorter sentences.

7 Which sentence is not stringy or choppy?
- [ ] a. Incorporating healthy foods, such as yogurt, into your diet is simple.
- [ ] b. Yogurt is a healthy food. You can include this in your diet. This can be simple.
- [ ] c. Yogurt is healthy, and it can be incorporated into a diet, and this can be done easily.

8 Which sentence is not stringy or choppy?
- [ ] a. The health benefits of potatoes, which are high in fiber, include disease prevention.
- [ ] b. Potatoes are a high-fiber food. Fiber is healthy. It can prevent diseases.
- [ ] c. Potatoes, which are a high-fiber food, can help prevent disease, and they also have other health benefits.

9 Which sentence is not stringy or choppy?
- [ ] a. Experts advise adults to eat breakfast every day. A busy schedule is no excuse. The morning meal is important.
- [ ] b. According to experts, adults should eat breakfast every day. Because the morning meal is so important, being busy is no excuse.
- [ ] c. Even though they know it is important, some people skip breakfast because they are busy, but they should still have something to eat in the morning.

10 Which sentence is not stringy or choppy?
- [ ] a. Tension is unhealthy. Try to eliminate it. Relax once each day. Doing something calming can have a positive effect.
- [ ] b. Because it causes stress, it is important to reduce tension, and since stress can be harmful to overall health, relaxation is vital.
- [ ] c. People who experience a great deal of tension should take steps to reduce it. They can find time to do a calming activity every day.

**Summarizing Outside Sources**

## CONNECTING TO THE THEME

Experts have written a lot about protecting personal information online. The most common recommendation is to be careful about who you share personal information with. Which sentence describes your approach to this idea?

**A** I never share my personal information online.

**B** I'm careful to only share personal data with trusted sites.

**C** I share my information any time I'm asked.

## A. Skill Presentation

To **summarize** a text from an outside source, give the main points of the original text and keep the overall meaning, but write it in your own words. Remember to:
- include the main points, but remove most of the details.
- use synonyms and different sentence structures to avoid plagiarism.
- make sure you did not change the writer's original meaning or add new information.

Look at this original text. Focus on the **main points**.

> [MP]One recent study on privacy shows that attitudes about it differ across countries and can be influenced by values within a society. Compare the United States and India. People in the United States tend to be uncomfortable when others have access to their personal information. In contrast, people in India may not be as worried if their personal information is accessible. [MP]For example, 82 percent of the Americans surveyed expressed concern about identity theft, compared to only 20 percent of Indians. [MP]Differences in social values is one factor that may explain these results. [MP]India is a society that tends to value the group over the individual. [MP]The United States, however, values the individual over the group.

Now read the summary. It includes only the main points from the original and uses different words and sentence structures.

> In general, opinions about personal privacy differ a great deal between the United States and India. A large majority of Americans believe that privacy issues such as identity theft are a concern, while only a few Indians share this view. One reason that attitudes differ may be related to values. Indians typically value the group over the individual, as opposed to Americans, who take the opposite view.

# B. Over to You

**1  Read the original text and the three summaries, and answer the questions.**

A survey was conducted in China to determine people's level of trust when using the Internet. It indicated that approximately 70 percent of Internet users do not trust information found on certain websites. The survey also revealed that approximately 62 percent believe companies use personal information obtained from websites inappropriately.

**Summary A**

A survey in China showed that many people do not feel secure when using the Internet. The survey indicated that approximately 70 percent of Internet users do not trust information found on certain websites, and 62 percent believe companies use personal information obtained from websites inappropriately.

**Summary B**

One survey revealed that the majority of people in China tend to mistrust information they find online. They are also likely to believe that companies misuse personal information collected online.

**Summary C**

A countrywide survey in China indicated that people do not always trust information they find on the Internet. They tend to believe that poorly written websites contain misleading information. The majority of people also assume that companies misuse personal information by selling it for a profit.

**1** Which summary is the best? ____

**2** Which summary uses much of the same wording as the original text? ____

**3** Which summary has changed the meaning of the original and added information? ____

**2  Read the paragraph and decide if each sentence is a main point that should be included in a summary or a detail that should not be included. Write *MP* for Main Point or *D* for Detail.**

[1]A survey was conducted last May to study Internet users' trust of information online. [2]Initial results indicate that about 60 percent of users do not trust information on many websites. [3]One reason for this is that business contact information may be missing. This can make a company appear untrustworthy. [4]For example, one company had a well-designed website. However, its lack of contact information made users suspicious. [5]Unprofessional-sounding names made other websites seem unreliable. [6]One such website, freevacationgiveaways.net, claimed to give travel advice. [7]A third reason for mistrust of some websites had to do with product descriptions. [8]One shopping website, for example, described a television as having "picture quality excellent with large screen of 1,000 inches!" While these results may not reflect everyone's attitudes on the Internet, they do give some idea of why many users approach the Internet with caution.

**1** ____     **2** ____     **3** ____     **4** ____     **5** ____     **6** ____     **7** ____     **8** ____

### Check!

**1** In order to summarize, include the main points from a piece of writing, but use _____ words.

**2** Include only the most important facts and keep the overall _____ the same as the original.

# C. Practice

**1** **Read the original sentences and the summaries. Decide if the summaries are appropriate or not, and check (✓) the correct box.**

**1** **Original:** The results of one Canadian survey reveal that dentists consider technology to be essential because it increases their efficiency.
**Summary:** Dentists in Canada believe technology is beneficial because it helps them work more efficiently.

☐ a. The summary is appropriate.
☐ b. The summary changes the original meaning.
☐ c. The summary copies wording from the original.

**2** **Original:** According to a recently published study, Japanese residents approve of laws that protect their personal information.
**Summary:** People in Japan approve of laws that protect their personal information.

☐ a. The summary is appropriate.
☐ b. The summary changes the original meaning.
☐ c. The summary copies wording from the original.

**2** **Read the original text and the summaries, and answer the questions.**

Research shows that Americans are growing more concerned about Internet privacy. One reason is that people now understand privacy issues better. Nevertheless, while people are concerned about online privacy, only 14 percent of Internet users read websites' privacy policies. Research shows that people of all ages worry about privacy. However, compared to adults, young people are less informed about privacy issues. Although they are aware of laws about privacy, the majority of adolescents do not fully understand these laws.

**Summary A**
Today, Americans are more concerned about privacy when using computers than they were in the past. Because more people are accessing the Internet, more people are reading privacy policies online. Furthermore, young people tend to be less concerned about privacy on the Internet because they are less informed about the many legal issues.

**Summary B**
Because understanding of privacy issues on the Internet has deepened recently, Americans' concern about these issues has increased. Although this concern is real, research reveals that very few people read privacy policies online. Furthermore, people of all ages are concerned about privacy on the Internet, but younger people tend to be less informed about the relationship between law and online privacy.

**Summary C**
Americans are growing more concerned about privacy issues on the Internet. One reason is that people now have a better understanding of privacy issues. Still, only 14 percent of Internet users read websites' privacy policies. Interestingly, people are equally worried about privacy issues, regardless of age. However, the majority of adolescents do not fully understand laws regarding privacy on the Internet.

**1** Which summary copies much of the wording from the original? ___
**2** Which summary changes the meaning of some of the original? ___
**3** Which summary is the best? ___

# D. Skill Quiz

**Check (✓) the correct answer for each item.**

1 A summary should
- [ ] a. make the overall meaning of the original clearer.
- [ ] b. provide details that the original left out.
- [ ] c. give the main points of the original.

2 When you write a summary,
- [ ] a. try to use words and phrases that do not appear in the original.
- [ ] b. change information as necessary to better suit your topic.
- [ ] c. copy words from the original to keep the meaning the same.

3 What can help you rephrase an original text using your own words?
- [ ] a. copy statistics from the original and provide appropriate citations
- [ ] b. replace words with synonyms and change sentence structures
- [ ] c. provide new examples to support your topic and add adjectives

4 Compared to the original text, a summary should be
- [ ] a. not as long.
- [ ] b. longer.
- [ ] c. the same length.

5 Choose the sentence that does not change the meaning of this text: *Laws dealing with Internet privacy vary in countries around the world.*
- [ ] a. Internet privacy laws are different in every state.
- [ ] b. Internet privacy laws differ from one country to another.
- [ ] c. People worldwide have different concerns regarding Internet privacy.

6 Choose the sentence that does not change the meaning of this text: *Many teenagers do not consider privacy issues when they use the Internet.*
- [ ] a. Teens are more likely than adults to post pictures online.
- [ ] b. Many teens do not know of laws to protect personal privacy online.
- [ ] c. Teens tend to use the Internet without thinking about personal privacy.

7 Choose the best summary for this text: *The Canadian government passed an act that controls the way companies can collect, use, and distribute personal information.*
- [ ] a. Canada passed an act to fund the collection, use, and distribution of personal data.
- [ ] b. Canada passed a widely supported law that prevents organizations from using personal data.
- [ ] c. Canada passed an act that regulates how personal data can be gathered, used, and shared online.

8 Choose the best summary for this text: *Germany has been one of the leading countries in the world in terms of Internet privacy issues.*
- [ ] a. Germany has provided clear guidance to its citizens about online privacy issues.
- [ ] b. Regarding Internet privacy issues, Germany has been an important global leader.
- [ ] c. In terms of Internet privacy issues, Germany has been one of the leading countries in the world.

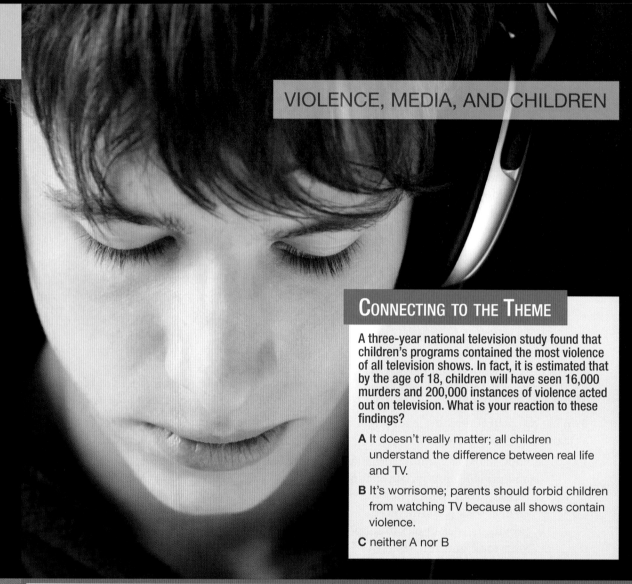

**Avoiding Overgeneralizations**

VIOLENCE, MEDIA, AND CHILDREN

## CONNECTING TO THE THEME

A three-year national television study found that children's programs contained the most violence of all television shows. In fact, it is estimated that by the age of 18, children will have seen 16,000 murders and 200,000 instances of violence acted out on television. What is your reaction to these findings?

**A** It doesn't really matter; all children understand the difference between real life and TV.

**B** It's worrisome; parents should forbid children from watching TV because all shows contain violence.

**C** neither A nor B

## A. Skill Presentation

An **overgeneralization** is a statement that is too broad or too general or a conclusion based on only a few examples. Overgeneralizations are imprecise, and often they are inaccurate. They frequently contain words such as *all* and *everybody*.

People believe that listening to music causes children to behave aggressively.

The statement is not accurate because it gives the reader the impression that *all* people believe that *all* music causes *all* children to behave aggressively. Now look at the words one writer added to correct the overgeneralization and make the sentence more precise.

**Many** people believe that listening to music **with violent lyrics** causes **some** children to behave aggressively.

Words such as *many*, *some*, and *often* can help correct overgeneralization. Supporting your ideas with plenty of details and examples and including facts from outside sources will also help you avoid overgeneralizations in your writing.

# B. Over to You

**1** **Read the sentences and check (✓) the one that is an overgeneralization.**

☐ a. *Recovery*, by American rapper Eminem, was the best-selling album in the United States in 2010.

☐ b. A 2010 study indicated that many parents worry about their teenagers listening to rap music.

☐ c. Listening to rap music causes violent behavior in teenagers.

**2** **Read each sentence in the chart, and decide if it makes an overgeneralization or not. Check (✓) the box in the correct column.**

| | OVERGENERALIZATION | NOT AN OVERGENERALIZATION |
|---|---|---|
| 1. Rap music affects listeners negatively. | | |
| 2. Rap songs tend to have violent lyrics. | | |
| 3. Anthropologist Sam Dunn states that some people incorrectly blame heavy metal music for violent acts. | | |
| 4. It is clear that heavy metal music causes everyone to act violently. | | |
| 5. Regardless of the lyrical content, music has no impact on behavior. | | |
| 6. In general, experts are unsure about the link between music and behavior. | | |
| 7. Many parents perceive lyrics in songs by the band Dead Kennedys to be violent. | | |
| 8. Although people enjoy rock music, it always contains violent lyrics. | | |
| 9. Dr. Wass, a psychologist, claims that 17 percent of teenagers listen to music with violent lyrics. | | |
| 10. Because parents disapprove of inappropriate music, every teenager loves it. | | |

---

## CHECK!

**1** Overgeneralizations are statements that are too general, or _____ based only on a few examples. They are _____, and often inaccurate.

**2** Overgeneralizations contain words like *all* and _____. Instead, use words like *many*, *some*, and _____.

**3** Avoid overgeneralizations in your writing by supporting your ideas with plenty of details and _____, and including _____ from outside sources.

# C. Practice

**1** **Read the paragraph about a rapper. It includes some overgeneralizations. Decide which of the numbered sentences / phrases make overgeneralizations, and which do not. Write *MO* for Making an Overgeneralization or *AO* for Avoiding an Overgeneralization.**

Starting in 2002, [1]Big Biz's music became extremely popular with teenagers. [2]In 2011, his rap album sold seven million copies – more than any other in the world. Big Biz was born in 1984 with the name Caleb Bismarck in Huntsville, Alabama. [3]He moved to Atlanta on his 18th birthday, with only $50 in his wallet. [4]Atlanta is a violent city. Big Biz writes songs about his life in Atlanta, and as a result, [5]some of his lyrics can be violent. In 2007, Big Biz was featured in the movie *Georgia Grit*. It is about a rapper trying to overcome challenges in his career. [6]All rappers have to overcome obstacles. The movie is not a biography of Big Biz's life, but there are some similarities. [7]Many of Big Biz's experiences influenced his music, and [8]his fans always support his success.

1 ___          2 ___          3 ___          4 ___
5 ___          6 ___          7 ___          8 ___

**2** **Match the overgeneralizations (1–6) with the corrections (a–f).**

___ **1** Women started the Parents' Music Resource Center (PMRC).

___ **2** Everyone agrees that lyrics should be printed on album covers.

___ **3** Members of one generation never like the music of the generation after them.

___ **4** In the past, no parents wanted their children listening to music.

___ **5** Parents hate music.

___ **6** Children do not care what their parents think of the music they listen to.

**a** In the 1950s, some parents did not want their children to listen to rock music.

**b** Some children listen to music that they enjoy no matter what their parents think.

**c** Twenty women who were married to senators started the Parents' Music Resource Center (PMRC).

**d** Like many other parents, members of the PMRC believed album covers should display lyrics to clearly indicate offensive language.

**e** For the most part, older generations tend not to enjoy the same music that younger generations do.

**f** There are parents who disapprove of some kinds of music.

# D. Skill Quiz

**Check (✓) the correct answer for each item.**

1 An overgeneralization is
- ☐ a. an extremely precise statement.
- ☐ b. a conclusion based on only a few examples.
- ☐ c. a fact that is repeated in several reliable sources.

2 One way to avoid overgeneralizations is to
- ☐ a. provide details and examples.
- ☐ b. make broad statements that seem to be true.
- ☐ c. delete words that add detail.

3 Which words help avoid overgeneralizations?
- ☐ a. all, everybody, everyone
- ☐ b. many, some, often
- ☐ c. always, never, is

4 Choose the word that makes this an overgeneralization: *Violent lyrics in music are a concern for all parents around the world.*
- ☐ a. violent
- ☐ b. music
- ☐ c. all

5 Choose the word that makes this an overgeneralization: *Despite the fact that some people are opposed to the band's lyrics, everyone wants to go to the concert.*
- ☐ a. everyone
- ☐ b. opposed
- ☐ c. some

6 Choose the best correction for this overgeneralization: *Parents hate violent lyrics in music.*
- ☐ a. All parents are concerned about violent lyrics in rap music.
- ☐ b. Parents in the Stop Violence group are opposed to violent lyrics in music.
- ☐ c. People with young children dislike song lyrics.

7 Choose the best correction for this overgeneralization: *Everyone wanted to go to the concert, but no parents approved of the band.*
- ☐ a. All teenagers wanted to go to the concert, but no parents approved of the band.
- ☐ b. Most teenagers wanted to go to the concert, but parents did not approve of the band.
- ☐ c. Many teenagers wanted to go to the concert, but very few of their parents approved of the band.

8 Choose the sentence that makes an overgeneralization.
- ☐ a. Some parents objected to Ozzy Osbourne's music in the 1980s.
- ☐ b. In the 1980s, Ozzy Osbourne had a large number of teenage fans.
- ☐ c. In the 1980s, everyone liked Ozzy Osbourne's music.

9 Choose the sentence that makes an overgeneralization.
- ☐ a. Music poses a threat to children and must be labeled with warnings.
- ☐ b. The Federal Communications Commission created labeling guidelines for CDs with explicit lyrics.
- ☐ c. Because some music is explicit, the CDs contain warning labels.

10 Choose the sentence that makes an overgeneralization.
- ☐ a. Tipper Gore and Susan Baker cofounded the PMRC in 1985.
- ☐ b. It is evident that no woman in the PMRC ever listened to music.
- ☐ c. The PMRC encouraged the use of warning labels on CDs with explicit lyrics.

**Avoiding Charged Language**

## CONNECTING TO THE THEME

Think about yourself and the way you study. Which option is closest to your approach?

**A** I multitask and study while I'm e-mailing or texting friends.

**B** I can't study unless there's music playing or the TV is on.

**C** I study alone in my room where it's quiet.

**D** I often study with a friend.

*If you answered A or B, you may suffer from information overload.*

## A. Skill Presentation

The best way to convince readers to agree with your ideas is to be as objective and impersonal as possible. In order to ensure this, you should avoid emotionally charged language.

One way to avoid charged language is to use neutral words. For example, instead of *wrong*, *stupid*, or *the best*, use words like *questionable*, *misguided*, or *important*.

His ideas seemed stupid at times. ✗
His ideas seemed misguided at times. ✓

Another way to avoid emotionally charged language is to provide clear examples to support your ideas and opinions. Look at these sentences. The writer has used neutral language and given an **example** to support his **opinion**.

[O]His ideas seemed misguided at times. For example, [E]he felt people were not working hard unless they were doing more than one thing at the same time. [C]Although multitasking may be one indication that people are working busily, it is often an inefficient way to accomplish tasks.

A third way to avoid emotionally charged language is to show that you agree with part of the opposing opinion. This lets your reader know that you have carefully **considered other points of view** before arriving at your own conclusion. For example, it is clear from the last sentence that the writer has considered an aspect of the opposing argument to be true but disagrees with the argument as a whole.

# B. Over to You

**1**  **Read the original emotionally charged sentence and the corrected sentence. Check (✓) the technique the writer used to make it more objective.**

**Original Sentence:** The professor's ideas about multitasking are ridiculous. Students who believe his theories are crazy.

**Corrected Sentence:** The professor's ideas about multitasking may not be based on actual research. It is possible that students who believe in his theories do not fully understand the issues.

☐ a. Emotionally charged words were replaced with more neutral words or phrases.
☐ b. The writer provided a fact to support the opinion.
☐ c. The writer indicated a potential area of agreement.

**2**  **Circle the more neutral words.**

**1** Multitasking while trying to learn something new is *unwise* | *stupid*.

**2** It is *problematic* | *outrageous* to assume that focusing on new information while checking e-mail and writing text messages is possible.

**3** The ability to absorb new information may be *ruined* | *limited* by multitasking.

**4** It is *misguided* | *ridiculous* to believe that multitasking is fundamentally better than doing just one task at a time.

**5** Because they are accustomed to multitasking in all areas of their lives, many students *dislike* | *hate* waiting until after class to check their text messages.

**6** Concentrating on schoolwork is important; therefore, it is *idiotic* | *risky* to study while watching television and talking on the phone.

**7** The belief that a student can read a magazine during class and retain the details of the lecture may well be *crazy* | *irrational*.

**8** Focusing on more than one thing at a time is *stupid* | *ill-advised* when the goal is to absorb new and complex information.

**9** People who multitask while learning tend to perform *poorly* | *horribly* on analytic test questions.

**10** Researchers at Toringville University conducted an *exciting* | *informative* experiment to study the effects of multitasking.

---

**CHECK!**

To avoid emotionally charged language:

**1** use _____ words instead.

**2** include clear examples and facts to _____ your ideas and opinions.

**3** identify areas where you may agree with the _____ opinion.

# C. Practice

**1** **Read the original sentences and suggested corrections. Check (✓) the best correction.**

**1** Multitasking is a useless technique for completing tasks effectively.

☐ a. People may believe they can get more accomplished by doing several things at once, but they are wrong. Multitasking is useless for completing tasks effectively.

☐ b. Although people may believe they can get more accomplished by doing several things at once, multitasking is not a very efficient way to complete tasks.

**2** Researchers have found that multitasking can actually have a terrible effect on the brain's learning processes.

☐ a. While it may seem that multitasking is harmless, researchers have found that it can actually have a negative effect on the brain's learning processes.

☐ b. While it may seem that multitasking is harmless, researchers have found that it has a disastrous effect on the brain's learning processes.

**3** The researchers discovered that multitasking kills the brain's normal learning process.

☐ a. The researchers discovered that multitasking negatively impacts the brain's normal learning process.

☐ b. The researchers discovered that multitasking destroys the brain's normal learning process.

**4** Relying on the part of the brain that does not store information for long periods of time is crazy.

☐ a. Relying on the part of the brain that does not store information for long periods of time is a horrible idea.

☐ b. Relying on the part of the brain that does not store information for long periods of time is unwise.

**2** **Read the sentences and decide which technique the writer included to make the writing objective and impersonal. Write *NL* for Neutral Language, *E* for Example, or *PA* for Partial Agreement.**

___ **1** Although multitasking may be effective when performing simple tasks such as making photocopies or organizing papers, it is not an ideal way to learn.

___ **2** Many mistakenly believe that multitasking means doing several things at once, but it is actually the process of quickly switching from one activity to another.

___ **3** The human brain is not capable of doing two tasks at once that require equal focus. A person cannot, for instance, read and understand an article while writing an effective essay about a different topic.

___ **4** Many teenagers make the questionable decision to do three or four things simultaneously rather than focus on one activity at a time.

___ **5** As a group, teenagers actually make more errors when they attempt to multitask, although they may get things done more quickly.

___ **6** Multitasking often introduces errors that could have been avoided by doing one task at a time. One study indicated that a teenager doing homework while talking on a cell phone made more errors than a teenager who performed each activity separately.

# D. Skill Quiz

**Check (✓) the correct answer for each item.**

1 The best way to persuade someone to agree with your opinion is to
- [ ] a. use emotionally charged language.
- [ ] b. state your opinion so strongly that it cannot be opposed.
- [ ] c. be impersonal and objective.

2 One way to maintain an objective tone is to
- [ ] a. cite sources carefully.
- [ ] b. use neutral language.
- [ ] c. avoid descriptive adjectives.

3 Another way to maintain an objective tone is to
- [ ] a. provide facts to support your opinions.
- [ ] b. present strong opinions using subjective language.
- [ ] c. avoid an overabundance of details.

4 Another way to maintain an objective tone is to
- [ ] a. explain why the opposite point of view is completely false.
- [ ] b. show that you agree with part of the opposing point of view.
- [ ] c. mention all the points of view that oppose yours.

5 Choose the sentence that is the most objective and impersonal.
- [ ] a. People are unwise to believe that multitasking is as efficient as doing one activity at a time.
- [ ] b. People are foolish to believe that multitasking is as efficient as doing one activity at a time.
- [ ] c. People are wrong to believe that multitasking is as efficient as doing one activity at a time.

6 Choose the sentence that is the most objective and impersonal.
- [ ] a. Teenagers should not multitask because they tend to make horrible mistakes when they do several things at once.
- [ ] b. Even though teenagers are better at multitasking than older adults, they tend to make horrible mistakes when they do several things at once.
- [ ] c. Teenagers may be better at multitasking than adults, but they tend to make more mistakes when doing several things at once.

7 How is the original sentence revised to make it more objective, impersonal, and persuasive?
Original: *The human brain is not capable of doing two complex tasks at the same time.*
Revised: *While it may be manageable to do two simple tasks at the same time, it is considerably more difficult to do two complex tasks simultaneously.*
- [ ] a. made language more neutral
- [ ] b. included an example
- [ ] c. included an area of agreement

8 How is the original sentence revised to make it more objective, impersonal, and persuasive?
Original: *For teenagers, multitasking may have negative effects on brain development.*
Revised: *For teenagers, multitasking may have negative effects on brain development. Some studies show that it can lead to poor critical thinking and analytical skills.*
- [ ] a. made language more neutral
- [ ] b. included an example
- [ ] c. included an area of agreement

## Elements of a Strong Argument

### CONNECTING TO THE THEME

Social networking has a strong educational value. Do you agree with this statement?

**A** No, I disagree because social networking is just that – social.

**B** Yes, I agree. Users gain access to a wide variety of opinions, and it also encourages creativity and the sharing of ideas – that's educational.

## A. Skill Presentation

The goal of many types of essays is to make a **strong argument** and convince the reader to agree with your point of view. There are many ways to make a strong argument.

First, write a strong thesis statement that clearly expresses the main point of the essay and conveys your opinion about the issue. Make sure you have chosen an issue that people could have different opinions about. In addition, the thesis statement should not be too general; otherwise, it will be difficult to provide appropriate support.

> Colleges and universities should block students' access to social networking sites because they waste students' valuable study time, and they are a distraction during class.

Another technique for making a strong argument is to include facts that are closely related to the essay topic and clearly support your thesis statement. Quotations will help make your argument stronger when they provide evidence that supports your opinions. Remember to tell the reader where the quotation comes from by including a reporting phrase, such as *According to*, followed by the exact words from the original text inside of quotation marks. Alternatively, use your own words to paraphrase ideas from the original source. Again, you must include a citation, but quotation marks are not needed. These techniques will help avoid plagiarism.

> According to Simon Callan, "More than 50 percent of students admit to logging on to social networking sites during class, and to spending at least 30 minutes each day checking for updates."

# B. Over to You

**1  Read the thesis statements and answer the questions.**

**A** There are many problems with websites.

**B** There has been a measurable increase in the use of social networking sites among college students in recent years.

**C** Colleges and universities should block students' access to social networking sites because they waste students' valuable study time, and they are a distraction during class.

| | | | |
|---|---|---|---|
| **1** Which statement is a fact and therefore has no opposing opinion? | **A** | **B** | **C** |
| **2** Which statement is too general? | **A** | **B** | **C** |
| **3** Which statement is the most effective? | **A** | **B** | **C** |

**2  Read each thesis statement in the chart, and decide if it is a strong statement or a weak statement. Check (✓) the box in the correct column.**

| | STRONG | WEAK |
|---|---|---|
| 1. Parents should block children's access to social networking sites because these sites do not protect privacy, and they encourage superficial relationships. | | |
| 2. A 2010 study showed that 15 percent of social networking site users in the United States were under age 17. | | |
| 3. Social networking has a strong educational value because it promotes collaboration between students around the world. | | |
| 4. Social networking sites are distracting for many people. | | |
| 5. Modern social networking sites have a number of drawbacks. | | |
| 6. Social networking sites are a revolutionary tool for change because they help people organize movements effectively and spread messages quickly around the world. | | |

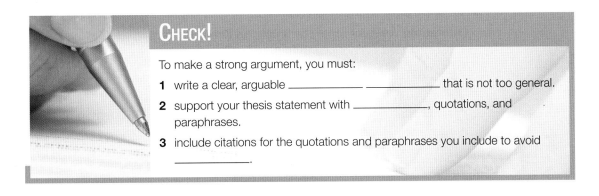

**CHECK!**

To make a strong argument, you must:

**1** write a clear, arguable _____ _____ that is not too general.

**2** support your thesis statement with _____, quotations, and paraphrases.

**3** include citations for the quotations and paraphrases you include to avoid _____.

# C. Practice

**1** **Read the sentences and decide if they express a fact or an opinion. Write *F* for Fact or *O* for Opinion.**

___ **1** The average user spends 5.3 hours per day on social networking sites.

___ **2** Social networking is an effective way for companies to reach consumers.

___ **3** According to one company, 77 percent of Internet users read blogs.

___ **4** People who are connected on social networking sites are not truly friends.

___ **5** Over 12 billion online videos are viewed every day in the United States.

___ **6** Eighty percent of U.S.-based companies use professional networking sites to find employees.

___ **7** A recent report confirmed that students get higher grades if they attend a college that blocks access to social networking sites.

___ **8** Most blogs contain superficial information that is not useful for researchers.

___ **9** Tablet computers offer instructional benefits that laptops do not.

___ **10** Event organizers should have relied on social networking sites to provide information to guests.

**2** **Read the original information and the way one writer has used it in an essay. Decide if each quotation or paraphrase is appropriate or not. Write *A* for Appropriate or *I* for Inappropriate.**

**1** More than 70 percent of visitors to the website live outside the United States. – Singleton Research

___ **Quotation:** According to Singleton Research, "More than 70 percent of visitors to the website live outside the United States."

**2** The majority of online video game players are women between the ages of 37 and 43. – Singleton Research

___ **Paraphrase:** Singleton Research concluded that the majority of online video game players are women between the ages of 37 and 43.

**3** Ads on social networking sites generate billions of dollars per year. – Singleton Research

___ **Quotation:** A recent report by Singleton Research states, "Ads that appear on social networking sites generate millions and millions of dollars per year."

**4** More than 200 million users access social networking sites from their phones. – Singleton Research

___ **Paraphrase:** A spokesperson from Singleton Research claims that more than 200 million users access social networking sites from their phones.

**5** One social networking site has been translated into over 70 different languages. – Singleton Research

___ **Paraphrase:** Singleton Research states that more than 70 different languages are used on a particular social networking site.

# D. Skill Quiz

**Check (✓) the correct answer for each item.**

**1** A good thesis statement for an essay that makes an argument

☐ a. provides general information that most people would accept as fact.

☐ b. is relatively specific, and others may disagree with it.

☐ c. contains several quotations that express opposing views.

**2** What is a fact?

☐ a. the way a person feels about a topic

☐ b. something that can be proven

☐ c. something one person believes

**3** What is a direct quotation?

☐ a. text with the exact wording as the original text

☐ b. information from a source that has been restated using different words

☐ c. an accurate summary of information from a source

**4** An acceptable paraphrase

☐ a. can change the meaning of the original sentence.

☐ b. can add information to the original sentence.

☐ c. does not change the meaning of the original sentence.

**5** Choose the most appropriate thesis statement for an argument essay.

☐ a. Some people believe that social networking sites can be dangerous for children.

☐ b. More than 30 percent of children have been contacted by strangers on social networking sites.

☐ c. Social networking may be unsafe for children who are not yet psychologically mature.

**6** Choose the fact.

☐ a. People spend too much time looking at photos on social networking sites.

☐ b. Looking at other user's profiles can become addictive since they contain interesting information.

☐ c. The average user spends approximately 1.5 hours per day visiting social networking sites.

**7** Choose the appropriate quotation of this information: *The most important factor in the group's success was the way they motivated team members.* – Tech News

☐ a. Tech News affirms that the most important factor in the group's success was the way they motivated team members.

☐ b. Tech News states, "The most important factor in the group's success was the way they motivated team members."

☐ c. According to Tech News, "one factor in the group's success was the way they increased team motivation."

**8** Choose the most appropriate paraphrase of this information: *The most important factor in the group's success was the way they motivated team members.* – Tech News

☐ a. Tech News reported that a key reason this group was successful was that they inspired other members of the team.

☐ b. According to Tech News, the most important factor in the group's success was the way they motivated team members.

☐ c. Tech News reports that this group won, and everyone who participated won something.

**abbreviation:** a shortened form of a word or phrase

**academic writing:** a kind of writing that is done in school; it usually includes more formal language than other kinds of writing (e.g., personal communication) and is impersonal (See Skill 3.)

**adjective:** a word such as *hungry*, *sweet*, or *good* that describes a noun

**appropriate source:** a source that contains factual and accurate informatio n; for example, a reference book, a newspaper, an academic journal, or a book written by an expert (See Skill 7.)

**argument:** the expression of an opinion supported by facts and examples; the purpose of an argument is to persuade the reader that the opinion is correct (See Skill 14.)

**cause–effect essay:** an essay that explains the reasons why an event or situation happens, or that gives the results of an event or situation (See Skill 2.)

**charged language:** strong language that elicits an emotional response; it may include words such as *hate*, *wrong*, *stupid*, or *the best* (See Skill 19.)

**choppy sentence:** a short, simple sentence (See Skill 16.)

**citation:** detailed information about an outside source of information used in a piece of writing; citations are necessary for quotations and paraphrases (See Skill 4.)

**clause:** a group of words that includes a subject and a verb

**coherence:** the clear organization of sentences in a piece of writing; putting sentences in logical order and using transition words and phrases are ways to create coherence (See Skill 2.)

**comma:** a punctuation mark (,) used, for example, to separate certain clauses in a sentence or to separate three or more items in a list

**comma splice:** two or more independent clauses connected only by a comma; it does not include a conjunction; this structure is considered incorrect and should be avoided (See Skill 1.)

**comparison essay:** an essay that compares two or more things; it shows how they are alike and/or how they are different (See Skill 8.)

**complex sentence:** a sentence with an independent clause and a dependent clause joined by a subordinating conjunction such as *after*, *because*, *if*, or *when*

**compound sentence:** a sentence with two independent clauses joined by a comma and a coordinating conjunction such as *and*, *or*, *but*, or *so*

**concise:** expressing only what needs to be said without using unnecessary words (See Skill 12.)

**concluding sentence:** a sentence that can restate the main idea in a paragraph, offer a suggestion, or make a prediction about the topic; it is often the last sentence in a paragraph (See Skill 5.)

**conjunction:** a word such as *and*, *or*, *but*, or *because* that connects single words, phrases, or clauses

**connector:** a word or phrase such as *for instance*, *both*, *because of*, or *consequently* that links ideas in a piece of writing and makes it more coherent; it can show similarities or differences or introduce new information; conjunctions are one type of connector (See Skill 2.)

**contraction:** a shortened form of a word or combination of words; it contains an apostrophe

**dependent clause:** a group of words that has a subject and a verb but does not express a complete idea; it cannot be used alone as a complete sentence

**descriptive adjective:** a word that helps create a detailed mental picture of a topic; it describes how something looks, feels, smells, tastes, or sounds

**detail:** a specific fact or piece of information

**direct quotation:** another writer's exact words (See Skill 10.)

**double quotation marks:** punctuation marks (") used before and after a direct quotation to show that the words are someone else's (See Skill 10.)

**essay:** a piece of writing with several paragraphs about one topic

**example:** something that illustrates a rule

**fact:** something that is true and can be proven (See Skill 14.)

**formal writing:** a style of writing used when it is not appropriate to show familiarity, such as in business or school; it may include full forms instead of abbreviations, or specific nouns instead of the pronoun *you*; it usually does not include informal expressions (See Skill 3.)

**full form:** the form of a word or group of words in which each letter appears; for example, *is not* is the full form of the contraction *isn't*

**inappropriate source:** a source that contains information that is not factual or not academic; for example, a newspaper that focuses on entertainment, a magazine that focuses on trends and celebrities, or a non-academic website like a personal blog (See Skill 7.)

**independent clause:** a group of words that includes a subject and a verb and expresses a complete idea; it can be used alone as a complete sentence

**informal writing:** a style of writing used with friends and family that is often based on personal experiences; personal e-mails or personal blogs are examples of informal writing (See Skill 3.)

**main idea:** what a piece of writing is about

**neutral language:** language that is impersonal or objective (See Skill 19.)

**noun:** a word for a person, place, thing, or idea

**object:** a noun that answers the question *What?* or *Who?* about the verb in a sentence; it comes after the verb in a statement

**objective:** not influenced by personal beliefs or feelings

**opinion:** someone's feeling or belief about a topic; it cannot be proven (See Skill 14.)

**opposing opinion:** an opinion that is different from a writer's own opinion (See Skill 15.)

**order of importance:** a way of organizing ideas according to their importance; for example, ordering ideas from most to least important or from least to most important

**overgeneralization:** a statement that is too broad or too general or a conclusion based on only a few examples; for example, it is an overgeneralization to say something specific about an entire group of people based on information about only one of the group members (See Skill 18.)

**paragraph:** a group of sentences about one topic; the sentences have a special format

**parallel structure:** the use of similar word patterns in lists of words, phrases, or clauses; for example, listing present tense verbs with other present tense verbs or listing prepositional phrases with other prepositional phrases (See Skill 6.)

**paraphrase:** to put another writer's idea or ideas in your own words (See Skill 4.)

**phrase:** a group of words

**plagiarism:** the use of another person's ideas or information without providing an appropriate citation. At colleges and universities in North America, plagiarism is a very serious offense; it is considered stealing. (See Skill 4.)

**preposition:** a word such as *in*, *on*, or *at* that helps show location or time

**prepositional phrase:** a preposition followed by a noun; for example, *at noon*, *in Boston*, or *on the table*

**pronoun:** a word that is used in place of a noun

**punctuation:** special marks that are used to show the divisions between phrases and sentences

**quotation:** another writer's exact words (See Skill 10.)

**quotation marks:** punctuation (") used before and after a quotation to show that the words are someone else's

**redundancy:** saying the same thing more than once, or repeating the same information (See Skill 12.)

**refutation:** a response to a counterargument; it brings readers back to the writer's original opinion and strengthens that opinion (See Skill 15.)

**repetition of words:** the frequent use of important words in a piece of writing (See Skill 11.)

**reporting phrase:** a phrase such *as according to*, *said*, *explained*, or *asks* that usually introduces a direct quotation; it often includes information about the source, such as the name of the author (See Skill 10.)

**revise:** to fix the overall problems with the structure of a piece of writing

**run-on sentence:** two or more independent clauses connected without a comma or a conjunction (See Skill 1.)

**sentence fragment:** a group of words that does not express a complete idea; a sentence fragment may be missing a subject or a verb, or it may be a dependent clause by itself (See Skill 1.)

**sentence structure:** the way words are arranged in a sentence

**sentence variety:** the use of sentences with different structures in a piece of writing (See Skill 9.)

**simple sentence:** a sentence with only one independent clause; it expresses only one complete idea

**single quotation mark:** a punctuation mark (') used around a quotation within another direct quotation (See Skill 10.)

**source:** someone or something from which a writer gets information

**stringy sentence:** a sentence that has too many clauses joined by connectors; it is often difficult to read (See Skill 16.)

**subject:** the person, place, thing, or idea that does the action in a sentence

**summary:** a brief statement that gives the main points of a piece of writing; it keeps the overall meaning of the original text but uses different words and includes only the most important points (See Skill 17.)

**supporting sentence:** a sentence that supports the main idea in the topic sentence; it can also give examples and explanations and may provide facts and details about the topic of the paragraph (See Skill 5.)

**synonym:** a word or phrase that has the same meaning, or nearly the same meaning, as another word or phrase (See Skill 4.)

**thesis statement:** a sentence that states the main idea of an essay; it should not be too broad and should express an issue that has two sides; it should make the writer's opinion clear (See Skill 20.)

**time clause:** a phrase that shows the order of events and begins with a time word such as *before*, *after*, *when*, *while*, or *as soon as*

**tone:** the general feeling expressed by a piece of writing; it can be formal or informal

**topic:** who or what a piece of writing is about

**topic sentence:** a sentence that expresses the main idea of a paragraph; it is often the first sentence in a paragraph, is about one idea, and does not usually include specific examples or details (See Skill 5.)

**transition phrases**: phrases such as *for example*, *as a result*, or *in conclusion* that link ideas between sentences and between paragraphs; they can also introduce new information and help organize ideas in a piece of writing (See Skill 16.)

**transition words:** words such as *first*, *therefore*, or *finally* that link ideas between sentences and between paragraphs; they can also introduce new information and help organize ideas in a piece of writing (See Skill 16.)

**verb:** a word that describes an action or a state; it tells what the subject in a sentence is doing or being

**wordiness:** the inclusion of unnecessary words in writing; it can make writing less clear and more difficult to read (See Skill 12.)

What are the most common words in academic English? Which words appear most frequently in readings in different academic subject areas? Dr. Averil Coxhead, who is currently a Senior Lecturer at Victoria University of Wellington in New Zealand, did research to try to answer this question. The result was the Academic Word List (AWL), a list of 570 words or word families that appear in academic readings in many different academic fields. These words are extremely useful for students to know. In *Skills for Effective Writing*, you will encounter a number of these words in context.

The following is a list of the AWL words in *Skills for Effective Writing 4* and the Skills where they appear.

| | | | | |
|---|---|---|---|---|
| abandoned | 10 | attitude | 17 |
| abstract | 6 | author | 7 |
| academic | 3; 7; 12–14; 16 | available | 4; 14 |
| academically | 14 | aware | 11; 13; 17 |
| access | 1–2; 15–17; 20 | beneficial | 5; 14–17 |
| accessible | 17 | benefit | 5; 14; 16; 20 |
| accuracy | 10 | bulk | 10 |
| accurate | 7; 10; 12; 15; 18; 20 | capable | 19 |
| accurately | 15 | challenge | 8–9; 18 |
| achievable | 9 | challenging | 2; 9; 13 |
| achieve | 2; 9; 12–14 | chart | 1–3; 7; 13–14; 16; 18; 20 |
| acknowledge | 15 | chemical | 1–2; 13 |
| adjust | 10; 16 | circumstance | 5 |
| administration | 14 | citation | 4; 14; 17; 20 |
| adult | 5–6; 14–17; 19 | cite | 9; 13; 19 |
| affect | 1–2; 5; 13; 16; 18 | clause | 1; 3; 6; 9; 12; 16 |
| alternative | 4; 9 | code | 8 |
| alternatively | 20 | coherence | 2; 8 |
| analytic | 19 | coherent | 2; 8 |
| analytical | 19 | colleague | 12 |
| annual | 11 | comment | 11 |
| appreciate | 4; 9; 14 | commission | 18 |
| appreciation | 9; 11 | communicate | 6; 8; 11 |
| approach | 12; 15; 17; 19 | communication | 3; 6; 8; 15; 18 |
| appropriate | 5; 7–8; 16–17; 20 | community | 3 |
| approximately | 3; 17; 20 | compatible | 12 |
| area | 10; 13; 19 | complex | 6; 9; 11; 16; 19 |
| aspect | 19 | complexity | 9 |
| assessment | 12 | compound | 9; 16 |
| assist | 5; 14 | computer | 2; 6; 8; 17; 20 |
| assume | 5; 17; 19 | concentrate | 19 |
| attain | 9 | conclude | 20 |

| | | | |
|---|---|---|---|
| concluding | 5 | design | 11–12; 14; 17 |
| conclusion | 8; 18–19 | despite | 5; 18 |
| conduct | 11; 17; 19 | discriminate | 15 |
| confirm | 20 | display | 10; 18 |
| conflict | 11 | distinct | 5 |
| consequence | 4–5; 16 | distribute | 16–17 |
| consequently | 2 | distribution | 17 |
| considerably | 19 | document | 7 |
| consistent | 12 | dominate | 12 |
| consistently | 12 | dynamic | 5 |
| constantly | 2 | economic | 9–10 |
| consult | 14 | economy | 3; 9 |
| consultation | 15 | element | 20 |
| consume | 14; 16 | eliminate | 16 |
| consumer | 2–4; 13–14; 20 | emphasize | 14 |
| consumption | 16 | energy | 4 |
| contact | 11; 17; 20 | ensure | 9–10; 19 |
| contemporary | 9 | environment | 1–3; 5; 8; 13 |
| contradict | 7 | environmentalist | 1 |
| contrast | 8; 17 | environmentally | 1; 3 |
| contribute | 3; 5; 12–13 | equipment | 3 |
| contributing | 4 | error | 7; 19 |
| contribution | 12 | establish | 10 |
| convert | 4 | estimate | 5; 18 |
| convince | 19–20 | ethical | 3 |
| co-operation | 1; 6 | evaluate | 3; 11; 15 |
| co-operative | 6 | evidence | 20 |
| corporate | 3 | evident | 18 |
| corporation | 3; 11 | expand | 5; 12 |
| create | 2; 4; 7–9; 13; 15–16; 18 | expert | 1; 5–7; 11; 13; 16–18 |
| creatively | 11 | explicit | 18 |
| creativity | 20 | expose | 13 |
| crucial | 11; 13; 15 | factor | 5; 17; 20 |
| cultural | 6; 8; 15 | feature | 18 |
| culturally | 2 | federal | 18 |
| culture | 7 | file | 1 |
| data | 2; 14; 17 | finally | 2–3; 8 |
| debate | 6 | finance | 3 |
| decline | 10 | financial | 8 |
| define | 7; 9 | flexible | 6 |
| defining | 7 | focus | 5–6; 17; 19 |
| definition | 9 | focused | 3 |
| demonstrate | 3; 6–7; 11–12 | found | 3 |

| | | | |
|---|---|---|---|
| founder | 3; 12 | involve | 11; 13 |
| fund | 3; 17 | involved | 3 |
| fundamentally | 19 | irrational | 19 |
| funding | 3 | issue | 3–4; 6; 12; 17; 19; 20 |
| furthermore | 17 | job | 6; 8–12; 14 |
| gender | 6 | journal | 7 |
| generate | 20 | justified | 3 |
| generation | 10; 18 | label | 13–14; 18 |
| global | 1; 4; 8; 11; 17 | labeling | 18 |
| goal | 2; 9; 11; 14; 19; 20 | labor | 10 |
| grade | 20 | lecture | 19 |
| grant | 10 | legal | 17 |
| guarantee | 9 | likewise | 8 |
| guideline | 1; 18 | link | 2; 8; 14; 18 |
| identify | 3; 6; 12; 15; 19 | locate | 13 |
| identity | 17 | location | 4 |
| ignore | 15 | logic | 12 |
| image | 7 | maintain | 9; 13; 19 |
| immigrant | 10 | maintenance | 14 |
| immigrate | 10 | major | 1; 6 |
| impact | 1; 3–4; 9; 18–19 | majority | 4–5; 12; 17; 20 |
| imprecise | 18 | mature | 20 |
| inaccurate | 15; 18 | media | 7; 18 |
| inappropriate | 7; 18; 20 | medical | 15 |
| inappropriately | 17 | medium | 9 |
| inconsistent | 7 | mentally | 15 |
| incorporate | 4; 16 | method | 1; 13; 15 |
| indicate | 6; 10–11; 13–14; 17–19 | migration | 10 |
| indication | 19 | modify | 13 |
| indicator | 12 | monitor | 15 |
| individual | 3; 5–6; 9; 11–12; 15; 17 | motivate | 16; 20 |
| input | 1 | motivation | 20 |
| instance | 2; 8; 18; 19 | negative | 2; 5; 12; 19 |
| institute | 7 | negatively | 4; 18–19 |
| instruction | 11 | networking | 20 |
| integral | 12 | neutral | 19 |
| intelligent | 13; 15 | nevertheless | 17 |
| interact | 11 | norm | 7 |
| interaction | 5 | normal | 19 |
| interpret | 6 | normally | 1; 5; 8 |
| invest | 16 | objective | 11; 14; 19 |
| investigate | 1 | obtain | 4; 17 |
| investor | 3 | obvious | 1 |

| | | | |
|---|---|---|---|
| option | 6; 9; 13; 19 | region | 1; 9 |
| outcome | 6; 12 | regulate | 17 |
| overall | 4; 16–17 | relax | 16 |
| overseas | 8 | relaxation | 16 |
| paragraph | 2; 4–6; 8–9; 11; 13–18 | relaxing | 16 |
| parallel | 2; 6 | relevant | 4–5; 7 |
| participate | 11; 14; 20 | reliable | 7; 10; 18 |
| participation | 4 | rely | 12; 19–20 |
| perceive | 18 | remove | 6; 12; 17 |
| percent | 1; 3; 5; 7; 10; 17–18; 20 | require | 1; 3; 12; 14–15; 19 |
| period | 2; 10; 19 | research | 2–3; 6–7; 11; 13–15; 17; 19–20 |
| physical | 9; 13; 15 | researcher | 6–7; 19–20 |
| physically | 15 | resident | 13; 16–17 |
| policy | 17 | resource | 4; 18 |
| pose | 18 | respond | 6; 11; 15 |
| positive | 2; 9; 12–13; 16 | response | 15 |
| potential | 11; 19 | restrict | 7; 15 |
| precise | 18 | retain | 19 |
| prediction | 7 | reveal | 13–14; 16–17 |
| previous | 5 | revise | 9; 11–12; 19 |
| primarily | 3; 8 | revision | 9 |
| primary | 4 | revolutionary | 20 |
| principal | 13 | role | 5; 9 |
| principle | 13 | schedule | 6; 8; 14–16 |
| prioritize | 14 | secure | 9; 17 |
| procedure | 15 | security | 9 |
| process | 3; 11–12; 19 | significant | 1; 6; 8; 12 |
| processing | 6 | significantly | 4; 8; 14–15 |
| professional | 9; 13; 20 | similar | 6; 8; 13 |
| project | 12 | similarity | 8; 18 |
| promote | 2–3; 20 | similarly | 8 |
| psychological | 12; 15 | simulate | 11 |
| psychologically | 20 | simulation | 11 |
| psychologist | 6–7; 18 | site | 1; 13; 17; 20 |
| psychology | 6; 12 | source | 1; 4; 7; 10; 13; 15–20 |
| publish | 7; 17 | specific | 2–3; 5; 12; 20 |
| purchase | 2–3; 9; 13; 15 | stability | 7 |
| pursue | 9 | statistic | 7; 17 |
| quotation | 7; 10; 20 | status | 10 |
| quote | 10 | strategy | 2; 3; 5 11 |
| random | 12 | stress | 14–16 |
| reaction | 3; 12; 18 | stressful | 11 |
| recovery | 18 | structure | 6; 17 |

| | |
|---|---|
| style | 4; 6–7; 12; 14 |
| substitute | 4; 15 |
| sum | 10 |
| summarize | 11; 17 |
| summary | 8; 10; 17; 20 |
| survey | 7; 17 |
| survive | 7; 14 |
| target | 2 |
| task | 5; 11–12; 14; 19 |
| team | 9; 11–12; 14; 20 |
| technique | 4; 9; 11–13; 19–20 |
| technology | 7; 17 |
| tension | 16 |
| text | 10; 16–17; 19–20 |
| theory | 12; 19 |
| thesis | 20 |
| topic | 2; 5–8; 14–15; 17; 19–20 |
| transfer | 4 |
| transition | 16 |
| transportation | 8 |
| trend | 7; 14 |
| unavailable | 5 |
| unethical | 15 |
| unique | 5 |
| unreliable | 17 |
| valid | 11; 12 |
| varied | 9 |
| vary | 5; 17 |
| vehicle | 4 |
| violate | 15 |
| virtually | 15 |
| visibility | 6 |
| vision | 6 |
| visually | 6 |
| whereas | 8 |